Becky—
So thankful to
work with someone
as caring as you!
Adam Rahn

CHATEAU STE. MICHELLE

THE FIRST 50 YEARS
1967–2017

Peter Blecha

HistoryLink / Documentary Media
Seattle, WA

CHATEAU STE. MICHELLE
THE FIRST 50 YEARS 1967-2017

Produced by HistoryLink and Documentary Media, Seattle

First Edition
Printed in China

HistoryLink
1411 4th Avenue, Suite 803
Seattle, WA 98101
Tel. 206.447.8140
admin@historylink.org

Documentary Media LLC
books@docbooks.com
www.documentarymedia.com
Tel. 206.935.9292

Author: Peter Blecha
Editor: Chris Boutée, Company B
Book Design: Paul Langland Design
Editorial Director: Petyr Beck, Documentary Media LLC

ISBN: 978-1-933245-47-8

Library of Congress Cataloging-in-Publication Data

Names: Blecha, Peter, author.
Title: Chateau Ste. Michelle : the first 50 years (1967-2017) / by Peter
  Blecha.
Other titles: Chateau Sainte Michelle
Description: First edition. | Seattle, Washington : HistoryLink, Documentary
  Media LLC, 2017. | Includes bibliographical references and index.
Identifiers: LCCN 2017002899 | ISBN 9781933245478
Subjects: LCSH: Chateau Ste. Michelle (Winery)--History. |
  Wineries--Washington (State)--Woodinville--History. | Wine and wine
  making--Washington (State)--History. | Riesling (Wine)--Washington
  (State)--History.
Classification: LCC TP557.5.W2 B55 2017 | DDC 663/.200979777--dc23
LC record available at https://lccn.loc.gov/2017002899

The vintage cork-screws featured throughout the book are part of a collection that has been handed down through the years at Chateau Ste. Michelle. The full collection is on display at the visitor center at the Chateau.

TABLE OF CONTENTS

FOREWORD

by Ted Baseler
President and CEO, Ste. Michelle Wine Estates

The 50th anniversary of Chateau Ste. Michelle gives us the unique opportunity to reflect back on the birth of the Washington wine industry and our journey over the past five decades to becoming one of the great wine regions in the world. We are proud of Ste. Michelle's role in launching an entire wine region and propelling the remarkable growth of the Washington wine industry.

Today, Washington is the nation's number two producer of premium wine with more than 60,000 planted acres, nearly 1,000 wineries, and 14 American Viticultural Areas or AVAs.

Few could have imagined when our early Washington wine pioneers planted the first grape vines in a remote, dusty corner of Eastern Washington that it would ultimately lead to Chateau Ste. Michelle becoming one of the leading domestic wine brands sold in the United States, with wines available in 100 countries.

This book is meant to share some of the stories of the people, places, and events that helped to shape the Washington wine region and Chateau Ste. Michelle winery. The writer conducted many interviews and researched numerous historical archives in an effort to bring these stories to life.

As proud as we are of what we have accomplished over the first 50 years, we can honestly say that the best is yet to come. Washington is poised for continuous growth and enhanced wine quality, with potential to plant thousands of additional acres of vines. The new Ste. Michelle Wine Estates Washington State University Wine Science Center will provide valuable viticulture research and educate talented winemakers and grape growers for decades to come.

We hope you enjoy this tribute to Washington wine and Chateau Ste. Michelle and develop a deeper appreciation for what makes Washington such an exceptional place to grow grapes and make world-class wines—and what it took to get here. We want to sincerely thank all those who have supported us along this journey, from past and present employees, growers, trade customers, distributor partners, loyal club members, and of course, our customers. We also thank our fellow Washington wineries for their amazing expressions of Washington wine and supportive community spirit. This is what makes the Washington wine community so special.

Cheers to the next 50 years of Washington wine!

Riesling grapes at
Viewcrest Vineyard

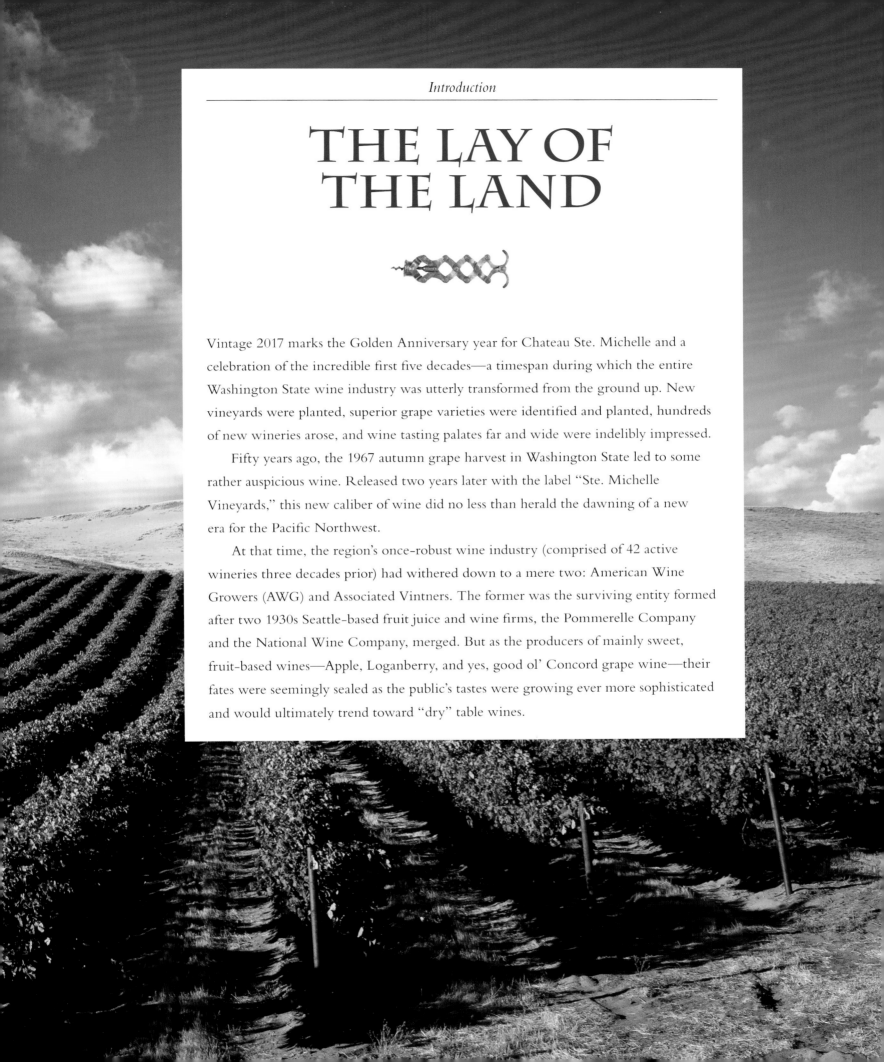

THE LAY OF THE LAND

Vintage 2017 marks the Golden Anniversary year for Chateau Ste. Michelle and a celebration of the incredible first five decades—a timespan during which the entire Washington State wine industry was utterly transformed from the ground up. New vineyards were planted, superior grape varieties were identified and planted, hundreds of new wineries arose, and wine tasting palates far and wide were indelibly impressed.

Fifty years ago, the 1967 autumn grape harvest in Washington State led to some rather auspicious wine. Released two years later with the label "Ste. Michelle Vineyards," this new caliber of wine did no less than herald the dawning of a new era for the Pacific Northwest.

At that time, the region's once-robust wine industry (comprised of 42 active wineries three decades prior) had withered down to a mere two: American Wine Growers (AWG) and Associated Vintners. The former was the surviving entity formed after two 1930s Seattle-based fruit juice and wine firms, the Pommerelle Company and the National Wine Company, merged. But as the producers of mainly sweet, fruit-based wines—Apple, Loganberry, and yes, good ol' Concord grape wine—their fates were seemingly sealed as the public's tastes were growing ever more sophisticated and would ultimately trend toward "dry" table wines.

Pommerelle's early
claim to fame:
Loganberry Wine

Although AWG operated from a modest building hidden away in industrial south Seattle, it was an ambitious company. As a predecessor of today's Chateau Ste. Michelle, its founders' original dreams have surely been more than realized. Not only would the company rise to become the Northwest's greatest winery, it also currently exists as the second-largest premium wine company in America. Along the way, it resettled into the historic Woodinville-based Chateau Ste. Michelle, one of the world's most-visited wineries.

The winding path taken to reach this level of success is a fascinating story that features forward-looking leadership, a commitment to quality, and a generous sense of community involvement. It required a deep respect for both the art and science that underpins the twin realms of viticulture (grape growing) and enology (winemaking). As true pioneers on the frontier of American wine, Chateau Ste. Michelle's corporate culture has long been one of embracing innovative practices and cutting-edge technologies, always seeking balance and improvement. The early decision to plant vineyards containing various *vitis vinifera* vines (native to Eurasia and preferred for winemaking for over 7,000 years), instead of sticking with locally traditional *vitis labrusca* grapes like Concord, has been proven correct. By striving endlessly to perfect its own wines, Chateau Ste. Michelle has helped raise the quality of Washington wines as well as the reputation of the region's winemakers.

American Wine
Growers, Inc. 1954
corporate license

A seminal Pacific Northwest brand, Chateau Ste. Michelle has been at the center of the action as the Washington wine industry has exploded over the past several decades. Today it is hard to believe that when the company launched its very first wines, the state of Washington had zero officially recognized grape growing "appellations" or AVAs (American Viticultural Areas). Today the state boasts *fourteen* AVAs: Yakima Valley (1983), Walla Walla Valley (1984), Columbia Valley (1984), Puget Sound (1995), Red Mountain (2001), Columbia Gorge (2004), Horse Heaven Hills (2005), Wahluke Slope and Rattlesnake Hills (2006), Snipes Mountain and Lake Chelan (2009), Naches Heights (2011), Ancient Lakes (2012), and Lewis-Clark Valley (2016).

Even more remarkably, within those AVAs there are now specific vineyards that—like certain esteemed vineyards in Europe—have achieved a level of prestige all their own, including Chateau Ste. Michelle's highly regarded Canoe Ridge Estate Vineyard, Cold Creek Vineyard, and Horse Heaven Vineyard. Together, the 60,000 current acres of vineyards in Washington supply grapes to nearly 1,000 Washington wineries, with a new winery opening about once a month.

Chateau Ste. Michelle's roots reach surprisingly deep into what is known as a rather new winemaking region. For five decades, it has been producing premier-level wines that have won untold numbers of medals and awards and captured the attentions of the wine world. First recognized as the greatest producer of Riesling wine in America, Chateau Ste. Michelle is now known for so much more. Yet the company remains focused on its foremost mission: to introduce consumers worldwide to prestige wines from Washington.

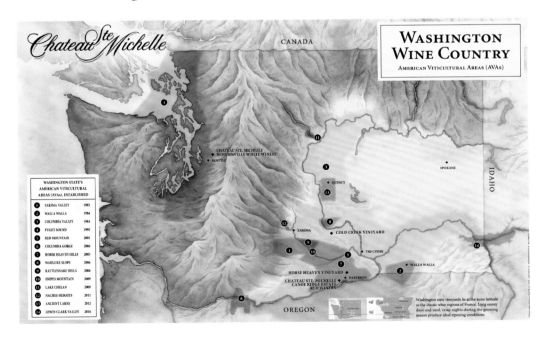

Ste. Michelle's vineyards are nestled in several of Washington State's AVAs.

Chapter One

BEGINNINGS

THE GRAPE COMES TO WASHINGTON

Well before anyone attempted to make wine in the Pacific Northwest, early visitors were transporting wine here. First came the Spanish and British explorers— most notably Captain George Vancouver and fellow officers aboard His Britannic Majesty's sloop-of-war *Discovery*. Historical records show they enjoyed the occasional bottle of wine while exploring Puget Sound as far back as May 1792. But imported claret is one thing; the challenge of growing grapes in this untested region and making wine from them is a whole other matter.

Wine grapes were—along with apples—the very first cultivated fruits in the Pacific Northwest. Initially planted here in 1827, both were cherished by early pioneering settlers. But whereas apples became a lucrative farm commodity early on, the grape's long and winding path to success was a bit rockier. Only in recent decades has both the art and science of viticulture and enology really advanced to the point where Washington-grown grapes and the wines made from them now enjoy global esteem for their excellence—an achievement in which Chateau Ste. Michelle played a leading role.

SEED TO VINE, GRAPE TO WINE

The first grapes cultivated here were grown at Fort Vancouver on the north bank of the Columbia River. This new fur trading post was built in 1825 by the British Hudson's Bay Company on a site selected by manager Dr. John McLoughlin, who thought that its flat terrain and fecund soil would support a farm that could feed his staff. Among the various fruits and vegetables planted were grapes and apples.

Both fruits came about as a lucky result of a visitor—probably the Hudson's Bay Company official George Simpson—on an inspection tour in November 1826. Legend holds that "A gentleman…while at a party in London, put the seeds of the grapes and apples which he ate into his vest pocket. Soon afterwards he took a voyage to this country and left them here, and now they are greatly multiplied." Likely planted during the spring season following Simpson's arrival, records show that the Fort was soon receiving shipments of corks and bottles along with other supplies.

TERROIR OF THE WASHINGTON TERRITORY

Showing off
grape bounty,
Eastern Washington,
circa 1925

The opening of the Oregon Trail brought the next wave of grape growing, as early emigrants hauled various grape cuttings to the region in their covered wagons. Among the first was Henderson Luelling who babied his vine cuttings all the way from Iowa in 1847. Although the Isabella variety of grape that Luelling brought was a native

North American (*vitis labrusca*) hybrid rather than the generally superior European (*vitis vinifera*) species of wine grape, the nursery that he and William Meek established in the Willamette Valley in 1847 helped other settlers get their homestead vineyards started.

In March of 1853 the northern portion of the Oregon Territories was officially split off as a distinct geopolitical entity, and the newly designated Washington Territory was born.

Its unique terroirs (soil types, topography, and climate conditions) were right for wine grape experimentation and planting by early settlers. By 1854 there were three active nurseries in the Puget Sound area that offered both *vinifera* and *labrusca* cuttings. The increased availability of these grape cuttings was especially welcome by members of the German, French, and Italian immigrant communities.

In 1859 William Meek's Isabella-based wine—among the very first documented from the Pacific Northwest—took an award at the California State Fair. About that same time, a Walla Walla-based baker from Lucca, Italy, Frank Orselli, began

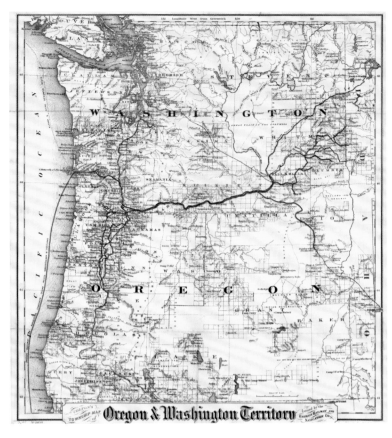

Oregon and Washington Territory map issued by Oregon Railway and Navigation Co.

making and marketing wine from his little California bakery. German immigrants joined in, too. Around 1861 Joseph Schanno and his sons planted grapes outside Union Gap in the Yakima Valley; in 1871 Anthony Herke planted them nearby at Tampico; in 1872 Phillip Miller planted grapes in Wenatchee, as did John Galler around 1873. French families were active, too, with Louis Delsol making Black Hamburg wine near the Washington/Idaho border by 1875, and Jean Marie Abadie producing as much as 550 gallons of wine in Walla Walla a year later. But judging from some of the unglamorous *labrusca* grapes these newcomers acquired—Niagara, Seneca, and Wyoming Red—and where on their properties they chose to plant them, it was more of a hit-or-miss approach to getting vines to take root and produce fruit.

On the western side of the Cascade Mountain range, Lambert Evans and Adam Eckert bought land on Stretch Island in the south Puget Sound area and began growing grapes Their *labrusca/vinifera* cross variety came to be known as "Island Belle," which served as the basis of the wine eventually fermented at the area's first commercial winery. Eckert promptly founded a nursery, selling plants and vines to homesteaders and farmers nearby and as far away as the Yakima Valley, just east of the Cascades.

LAMBERT EVANS & ADAM ECKERT

Washington State's first commercial vineyard was founded by Confederate Civil War veteran Lambert B. Evans. After the war, Evans headed West with grapevine cuttings in his knapsack. He arrived in Olympia, Washington, in 1872 seeking productive farmland. A southeasterly sloping hillside along the bank on Stretch Island in the southern waters of Puget Sound caught his eye. The water access and sun exposure looked ideal for growing fruit. Evans acquired 172 acres and began planting apples and grapes.

Historic vineyard on
Stretch Island, 1943

In 1899, businessman and distillery owner Adam Eckert came to the island from the "Chautauqua Grape Belt" area of Auburn, New York. As a wine enthusiast, he was excited by Evans' success at growing grapes in the area's moderate climate. Evans sold the newcomer 40 acres of land and Eckert planted black *vitis labrusca* ("Campbell Early") vines he had acquired from back East. It turned out that these vines were very well suited to the area's terroir and their Concord-like grapes were easy to crossbreed. Before long Eckert had developed a unique strain—one that deserved its own name. Eckert family lore holds that the name was inspired by one of his daughters, Lottie Eckert, whose attendance at a community dance caught everyone's attention, making her the "belle of the ball." Thus, Stretch Island became the home of the popular Island Belle varietal grape.

THE YAKIMA VALLEY

The Yakima River made it possible to transform the Yakima Valley's scrub-brush desert into a bountiful agricultural area. Early settlers were quick to test the rich volcanic-ash soil's potential for grapes. In 1891, the Sunnyside Canal irrigation project helped accelerate agricultural growth in the valley. A decade later, Seattle real estate developer Elbert F. Blaine settled into the town of Grandview and—as the manager of an irrigation company—was soon touting the possibilities of a serious grape growing and winemaking industry in the area.

The United States Bureau of Reclamation began a series of irrigation projects in 1905 that facilitated the launch of a new wave of grape vine plantings. Blaine eventually produced wine from varieties (including Concord) at his Stone House Winery near Grandview, Washington. That *labrusca* grape would be the one that would come

Harvest time in Yakima

Valley, circa 1910s

to define Washington grape growing—and even winemaking to a significant extent—for decades to come. First planted here in 1904, Concord had long been a popular table grape also used for making jellies, jams, and juice.

Other wine enthusiasts, especially members of the Italian, French, and German communities who prized more traditional grapes like Zinfandel, Cabernet Sauvignon, and Riesling, still had to source those grapes from out of the region. The "California grape train," which arrived in Seattle's industrial Georgetown neighborhood each fall after the harvest, supplied this growing demand.

WILLIAM BRIDGMAN

In 1902 a young Canadian lawyer and ex-school teacher named William B. Bridgman rode his horse-drawn wagon into the Yakima Valley farming town of Sunnyside, Washington, and set to work managing a small irrigation company. Bridgman also did some research into the climate and conditions of the valley compared to wine growing regions of California and traditional wine climates in Europe. "He concluded that the Yakima Valley climate is better for winegrowing than that of central France, having more days of sunshine, and noted that its latitude (46 degrees north) is midway between the latitudes of Burgundy and Bordeaux. This convinced Bridgman that Washington could grow finer European grapes than California could."[1]

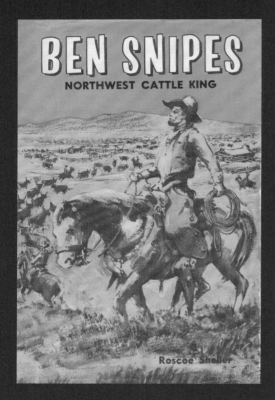

Snipes biography, 1957

Bridgman acquired some prime land on Harrison Hill at the southwest edge of Sunnyside and planted a portion of it to table grapes in 1914. Three years later he planted a few different *vinifera* varieties in a second vineyard situated nearby on Snipes Mountain, named after the local 1850s cattle baron, Ben Snipes. Washington State had just enacted anti-alcohol Prohibition laws in 1916. With wine now unavailable at stores, people were opting to make their own, creating a spike in demand. Bridgman's "foresight was rewarded by an increased sale of wine grapes, at prices far greater than his neighbors received for table varieties."[2]

By the end of Prohibition in the 1930s, Bridgman had planted over 165 acres of grapes. He founded the Upland Winery in 1934, producing 7,000 gallons of wine in its first season. Yet despite a promising start, Bridgman and other growers lost most of their vines to savagely cold winters in 1949 and again in 1950. He forged on, but by 1962 Bridgman had sold both the Upland Winery and Harrison Hills vineyards. In the end, "Bridgman's long-standing faith in the potential for growing grapes and producing fine wines in Washington had fallen before the economic realities of his era and the absence of enough varietal and cultural information on how to grow *viniferas* in Washington."[3]

But a major upheaval in the regional wine industry interceded, first with alcohol Prohibition in 1916 and then with the repeal of those restrictions in 1933–34. Immediately upon Repeal, a wave of applicants stepped up to register, or "bond," their new wineries with the government. First among them was St. Charles Winery, based at Lambert Evans' old homestead and vineyards along Puget Sound. On the eastern side of the Cascades, the first was William Bridgman's Upland Winery in Sunnyside—a site that Ste. Michelle president Wally Opdycke would later consider purchasing as a potential base for his planned winery. Thanks to the *vinifera* grapes he had planted, Bridgman was also the first to commercially market a European-style wine.

Rare promotional poster for Pommerelle, one of the first two Seattle-area wineries opened post-Prohibition

The first two Seattle-area wineries of the post-Prohibition era would make a big impact: one founded by a group of German Americans, the Pommerelle Wine Company, and the other founded by Italian Americans, the National Wine Company. The Chateau Ste. Michelle story comes into focus with the success and merger of those two companies, eventually forming one of the greatest wine enterprises in the world.

Winemaking for the National Wine Company, a predecessor to Ste. Michelle, late 1930s

DEEP ROOTS

THE WASHINGTON WINE INDUSTRY

*The roots of Chateau Ste. Michelle reach back to the very beginnings
of the commercial wine industry in the Pacific Northwest.
Indeed, the company evolved from a pairing of two of the earliest wine-producing
firms of the post-Prohibition era.*

REPEAL AND THE STEELE ACT

The adoption of the Twenty-First Amendment to the Constitution on December 5, 1933, ushered in a new era of legalized alcohol production and consumption, albeit with a slew of new rules and regulations. That very same month the Washington State Legislature convened an unusual session to consider Senator Earl Steele's Senate Bill 7. Passed into law, the Washington Liquor Act (R.C.W. Title 66), commonly called the Steele Act, "established a comprehensive structure for state regulation of the sale of liquor and created a three-member state Liquor Control Board."[4]

In the immediate wake of Repeal, about 42 wineries were founded. The first was Charles "Bill" Somers' St. Charles Winery on Stretch Island in south Puget Sound. The Pommerelle Company and the National Wine Company soon followed. Surprisingly, most of these new wineries were based west of the Cascade Mountains. And they were not alone. "Almost overnight, everyone in Washington with so much as a berry patch wanted to build a winery," quipped Leon D. Adams, the famed Sausalito-based wine expert and founder of the Wine Institute, in his book, *The Wines of America*.[5] But it was certainly no joke that wines were now being made from locally grown berries, apples, and grapes and that these local sources would drive the industry more and more over the next three decades.

CHARLES SOMERS

Old St. Charles
Winery sale brochure

The old Lambert Evans farm was purchased from his widow in 1918 by Charles Somers, a Seattle real estate agent. During Prohibition Somers did a roaring business selling home winemakers Island Belle grapes. Within days of the Repeal of Prohibition, Somers registered a winery with the government. His St. Charles Winery was Washington's first bonded winery. Both his sons, Charles "Bill" Somers and Howard Somers, joined him and learned the trade. St. Charles produced 100,000 gallons per year at its peak, and continued wine production up until around 1965 when it was purchased and closed by Alhambra Wine Company in Selah, Washington.

THE POMMERELLE CO.

Seattle's first winery was the Pommerelle Company, founded in early 1934 by a half-dozen largely German American investors, including: Dr. William Leede

Pommerelle Winery,
716 Dearborn Street,
1937

(Seattle physician); August Buschmann (Alaska fish industry scion); Fred Wonn (Eastern Washington orchard operator); Wilhelm L.H. Braiks (investment manager and Dutch Consulate employee); A. Vanderspek (investment manager and Holland America agent); and a Mrs. Pfisterer (office administration). Soon, they added John "Joe" G. Molz as manager, while Braiks served as president. Vanderspek's son-in-law, John Kangley, was their inaugural winemaker, but soon enough Molz took over that role— and in time, Carl Heinrich Kroll would be added as bottling and shipping manager.

Their business was launched in the bottom floor of a vacant former hotel building at 617 Dearborn Street—just north of Seattle's Chinatown District (today's International District). The former meat-processing and smoking firm was refitted with new redwood fermentation tanks and winemaking equipment.

Molz was a German immigrant who had privately been making his own apple juice for years, so it was easy for him to switch to producing "hard cider" and then apple wine, which was sold under such brands as Old Smiley, William Tell, and Butch 21/21. By 1935 Pommerelle—whose name derived from the French term for *little apple*—was marketing apple juice, apple wine, and Pommerelle Extra Dry with the slogan, "Finer Wines For Thrifty Hospitality."

Business was so good that the company was able to acquire a used Kenworth delivery truck formerly owned by the Frederick & Nelson department store. In 1938 Pommerelle relocated to an even larger facility at 9417 East Marginal Way—the very same building that Ste. Michelle Vintners would launch from over 30 years later. It was not exactly a romantic spot, wedged between

Rare Pommerelle berry wines promotional poster

a slaughterhouse holding pen, Isaacson Steel, a Duwamish River sawmill, and the Boeing Field airport. The business grew and Molz rented a warehouse that had its own railroad spur to facilitate storage and shipping.

In 1940 and '41 the plant was enhanced with the construction of a distillery tower, brandy storage, and fortifying facilities. As the company expanded, so did their fruit holdings. Pommerelle acquired a small berry farm at Deer Lake on Whidbey Island then purchased Greenbank Farm, a 500-acre dairy property on the island. Before long the company had planted 125 acres of loganberry bushes, which began Pommerelle's long practice of marketing berry wine.

THE NATIONAL WINE COMPANY

Founded in 1935 by a group of mainly Italian American Seattle businessmen, the roots of the National Wine Company (NAWICO) trace back to 1932, when the grape importers, Philip and Frank Sugia, and some friends rented a garage just below Queen Anne Hill near the Fremont Bridge and started making *sub-rosa* wines. Along the way, a few other interesting characters entered the picture, including Dominic Depaolis, bootlegger and subsequent alcohol distributor, and Frank M. Alvau, the experienced still-builder who had been convicted back in 1928 of violating the [national] Prohibition act, but was later let off on appeal. Joining them over time were Joe Carbonnato, Virgil Layton, Dominic Cappellaro, Sivilio Poli, and James "J.C." Sams.

By 1935 the Sugias had been bought out and the small operation was recast and formally bonded by the state as the National Wine Company, with Dominic Depaolis serving as president, Frank Alvau as secretary, and J.C. Sams—who came aboard with "the knowledge and experience of many years in the brewing field"— as general manager.

The young company thrived initially via the grapevine, as their advertising campaign for several years largely amounted to adopting the slogan "Washington's Finest" and buying modest classified ads in local newspapers which simply asked fans to "Call for NAWICO wines at cafés, clubs, beverage stores." Among their popular products were Apple Andy ($1.32 per gallon) and Loganberry

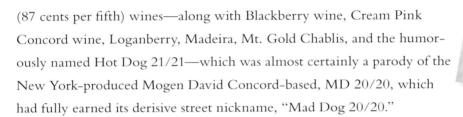

HOT DOG

IT CUTS THE MUSTARD

(87 cents per fifth) wines—along with Blackberry wine, Cream Pink Concord wine, Loganberry, Madeira, Mt. Gold Chablis, and the humorously named Hot Dog 21/21—which was almost certainly a parody of the New York-produced Mogen David Concord-based, MD 20/20, which had fully earned its derisive street nickname, "Mad Dog 20/20."

It was reportedly J.C. Sams who drove NAWICO's efforts to improve their processes and products. "With quality his paramount objective, [Sams] not only sought in every way to improve his own company's wines, but also cooperated in bettering the standards of all Washington-made wines." The company's early interest in strict quality control won them critical kudos as it "thus has enabled this state's winemakers to achieve in a relatively few years a quality of product considered comparable to the finest anywhere. And it is to a concentration on quality that the National Wine Co…attributes its rapid rise to a position of eminence among Washington winemakers."[6]

That rise in prominence also called for an expansion in NAWICO's infrastructure. In addition to their bottling plant at the Nickerson Street location in the Fremont neighborhood, the group built a grape processing plant and fermenting cellar in the Yakima Valley agricultural town of Grandview. That same year they hired a local fellow, Les Fleming, to help install wooden tanks and a copper still at the new facility, which were put into operation for the 1938 fall crush. Fleming ended up managing the winery and its associated vineyards through the 1970s. One of his first moves was hiring his friend Victor "Vic" Allison, who worked next door at the Wright Winery. It was a good hire: Fleming focused on the vineyards, while Allison managed the NAWICO Winery. Over the next few years, they built the firm into a $100,000-a-year operation.

NAWICO marketed wines without much old world finesse as late as the 1970s.

Les Fleming taking pride in a job well done

NAWICO crew
making wine at
Grandview winery,
late-1930s

THE WASHINGTON WINE
PRODUCERS ASSOCIATION

The first attempt to organize the state's wine producers occurred in 1935 with the formation of the Washington Wine Producers Association (WWPA). Interestingly, that same year brought about governmental changes that would affect the industry for decades—both positively and negatively—across the commercial and political landscape. An amendment to the 1933 Steele Act was passed by the Washington State Legislature, resulting in a near monopoly (for importing out-of-state wines) being granted to Washington State's own string of liquor stores. If wholesale distributors or individual grocers wanted to stock any such wines, they could go to one of those government-run shops to acquire them—but they would be paying the Washington State Liquor Control Board's retail prices before adding their own profit margin on top of that. By default, this meant that countless grocery stores across the state would choose to acquire their stock from in-state wineries.

While the change angered outside wineries whose access to local consumers would be curtailed, it offered a form of protection to Washington's active wineries. The WWPA must have been quite pleased—and perhaps never even imagined that a legal struggle with various California wineries would one day challenge this new

WASHINGTON WINE COUNCIL
Quality Wines
PRODUCED BY MEMBER WINERIES

arrangement. Meanwhile in 1938, the WWPA reorganized itself as the Washington Wine Council—an organization to which NAWICO's J.C. Sams would be elected president for seven consecutive years.

WINE SCIENCE

Experienced grape growers—farmers as well as industrial professionals—had long been accumulating an understanding about fundamental agricultural issues such as: general temperature ranges and prevailing wind patterns in their area; the topographic

contours of their land; the pH, nutrient levels, and texture of their soil; and matters of drainage and water accessibility. But a truly disciplined and exacting scientific approach to studying such key factors was still needed to achieve excellence.

The center of early grape-related science in the Pacific Northwest was Washington State University (WSU), which was originally founded in 1892 as the Washington Agricultural College and School of Science in Pullman, Washington. In 1919 the state legislature established the Irrigation Experiment Station (today's Irrigated Agriculture Research and Experimentation Station) in the farming town of Prosser, with a mission "to discover and disseminate scientific knowledge that enhances the competitiveness of irrigated culture."[7]

Over the decades dozens of WSU-based scientists would contribute greatly to the advancement of the wine industry's eventual understanding about grape varieties, soil types, pest control, irrigation, and other important issues. Two faculty members in particular, Dr. Walter J. Clore and Dr. Charles W. Nagel, have earned the highest

THE MISSOULA FLOODS

The finest vineyard sites in Washington and around the globe have earned their status in large part based on their particular terroir. Various aspects of each vineyard's specific geographical setting and natural environment (including the general climate, the land's topography, and soil type) are significant factors in the quality of grapes grown in that habitat and the wines that come from it. Soil type is key to the characteristic flavors imparted to a wine. The soil found in many vineyards in Eastern Washington has proven to be ideal for grape growing and owes its physical makeup to a number of cataclysmic climatological and geological events that occurred more than a dozen millennia ago.

In the 1920s geologists began unraveling the mysteries of exactly how the huge canyons in Eastern Washington—including the 900-foot deep Grand Coulee—had been gouged out of solid volcanic lava fields. Their research led to a theory that at the end of the last Ice Age (around 14,000 years ago), a giant glacial lake had formed behind a 23-mile-wide ice dam in what is now the state of Montana. When that dam eventually broke, Lake Missoula (and another, Lake Columbia, which covered much of the greater Spokane area) swept across the scabland in a series of massive outpourings dubbed the Missoula Floods. Those ancient hydrodynamic incidents scoured the land thoroughly, washing away topsoil and leaving behind the various canyons, coulees, buttes, plateaus, and river gorges seen today. They also, thankfully, left behind deep deposits of rock, gravel, silt, and other sediments carried from distant lands. Those deposits, low in nutrients and well draining (which stimulates deep root structure in grape vines), serve as the geological base for Washington's wine industry.

Missoula Floods left a stark and harsh landscape, photo circa 1947

praise for their contributions to the expansion of knowledge about local growing conditions. Their early work has been followed up by many researchers including agricultural engineers, climatologists, enologists, entomologists, food microbiologists, horticulturists, plant pathologists, and soil scientists. These experts have "worked to solve the problems of cold hardiness and efficient vineyard management, trellising and mechanical harvesting, certification of virus-free stock and testing of hundreds of grape varieties, balance of sugars and acidity in wines, and consumer preferences. Their research results were shared with growers, processors, and winemakers."[8]

DR. WALTER J. CLORE

The "Father of the Washington State Wine Industry" was born in Oklahoma in 1911 and later earned a Bachelor of Science degree in horticulture from Oklahoma State University in 1933. "Walt" Clore took a job at Washington State University the following year, and in 1937 began serving as an Assistant Horticulturist at the Irrigation Experiment Station in Prosser, where he got "involved with research on apples, pears, cherries, peaches, asparagus, beans, corn, chrysanthemums, peonies, and roses, as well as grapes—anything that might grow in irrigated central Washington."[9] In one of history's ironic little plot twists, Clore, who had been raised in a teetotaling Methodist household, had never tasted a single drop of wine before arriving here. By 1950 his work focused mainly on asparagus and *vitus labrusca* grapes grown locally for common fruit juice.

Dr. Walter Clore,

1984

But Clore's studies would lead him to becoming "the leading force in the transformation of vineyard practices—trellising, training, pruning, and watering in relation to mechanical harvesting, vine maturity, and cold hardiness—to suit the climate of the state."[10] Clore subsequently befriended vineyard owner William Bridgman, who gave him a few vine cuttings and pushed him to take on the study of more varieties of hybrid grapes—both *vitis labrusca* and *vitis vinifera*. It was around 1941 when Clore began experiments with twenty *labrusca* varieties, along with seven *vinifera* varieties, but over the next half-decade those totals would expand to more than 45 *labrusca* and 71 *vinifera* rootstock species. After Clore's *The Wine Project* was launched in 1964, those numbers exploded, with over 312 different varieties being planted at the research center at Prosser.

Clore developed a keen sense of which areas might be best for growing which types of grapes, and he became the go-to guy whenever anyone was considering planting new vineyards. At a time when most *labrusca* wines were of less-than-stellar quality, Clore "had the idea that better grapes could be grown and better wine made, and as a faculty member he had both the freedom and the obligation to pursue research that would ultimately prove of great value to the state of Washington."[11] Over time Clore assisted many young wineries, including Seattle's American Wine Growers and Associated Vintners.

After retiring in 1976, Clore remained an in-demand expert for many years. His four decades of service in the industry contributed immeasurably to the planning of many of the finest local vineyards, and in time the Legislature would see fit to declare him the Father of the Washington State Wine Industry. Upon his passing in 2003, Washington State Senior Senator Patty Murray entered her tribute to this great pioneer of Washington wine into the Congressional Record. It read in part that Dr. Clore "pursued his passion with unrelenting determination and transformed his vision of a vibrant Washington wine industry into a reality." To further honor his lifetime of work, the Walter Clore Wine and Culinary Center opened in 2014. The center is a 17,537-square-foot educational facility and tourist destination situated on a 22-acre site in Prosser, Washington, adjacent to the Yakima River.

The Walter Clore
Wine & Culinary
Center, 2014

DR. CHARLES W. NAGEL

Dr. Charles Nagel

In 1964 Dr. Walter Clore recruited a Washington State University microbiologist and assistant professor of horticulture named Dr. Charles "Chas" Nagel. Nagel had been raised in California's Napa Valley, where his father was a grape grower and had been employed at the Louis M. Martini winery. Nagel picked grapes as a boy and eventually got into the business as a cellarman at the Charles Krug operation. Nagel had also earned his Ph.D. at the University of California, Davis, along with a minor in the field of food science. As winemaker Mike Wallace said in Nagel's obituary, his "research on the chemical composition of Washington wines helped identify which grapes could most successfully be grown in the state, and his studies on fermentation research led to the production of more complex wines."[12] Nagel's expertise with sensory evaluation was also invaluable to the budding industry: "His greatest contributions to the development of the Washington wine industry were the introduction of trained wine tasting panels to evaluate wines from the educated consumer's viewpoint and his scientific work on identifying and correcting problems to improve the quality of the wines."[13]

CONSOLIDATING AND EXPANDING

The low-key, cross-town rivalry between the National Wine Company (NAWICO) and Pommerelle had been ongoing since day one, but in 1940 NAWICO presented Pommerelle with the opportunity to buy them out. Fred Wonn negotiated the sale to Pommerelle and the two companies henceforth carried on as teammates, each working their different markets. Meanwhile, WWII broke out, bringing with it years of material shortages, supply rationing, and a temporary industry-wide sales slump that caused numerous other wineries, both locally and nationally, to shutter their doors.

Yet NAWICO forged on. Over the next decade its Grandview facility tripled in size, the employee roster grew to forty-some workers, and company leadership focused on improving quality by sourcing the best grapes possible. NAWICO decided the best way to do that was to own and operate their own vineyards. The company continued to buy vineyards in the Grandview area as well as buy out the harvests of local growers they thought had the best quality grapes.

In 1951 Vic Allison introduced the first commercial plantings of European *vinifera* grapes in Washington on NAWICO's Columbia Valley acreage. The grapes were of the French Rhône Valley variety, Grenache, and Allison has long been credited as a guiding light and pioneer in the production of premium table wines in this state. By 1953 Pommerelle was also acquiring grapes from what was described as Washington's "Maryhill District" above the Columbia River.

NAWICO wines featured prominently (if not elegantly) in a local Thriftway store, circa 1950s.

AMERICAN WINE GROWERS

In 1954—twenty years after the founding of the Pommerelle Wine Company—NAWICO's J.C. Sams was in charge and formally merged the two associated wineries with a third Seattle entity, Italian Winery, creating the new American Wine Growers (AWG) firm, which opted to keep the two main company names alive as separate brands.

Pommerelle Manager Joe Molz steadily brought in new talent including, as a consultant, the one local person perhaps most identified with wine culture, University of Washington Professor Emeritus of English, Dr. Angelo Pellegrini. Italian born and Washington raised, Pellegrini was a well-known local aesthete and raconteur who had published his debut book, *The Unprejudiced Palate*, back in 1948. He also penned the popular "Notes on Enjoyment of Bread and Wine" column for the *Seattle Post-Intelligencer* and in 1965 would publish his classic *Wine and the Good Life*.

Pellegrini was a perfect fit for AWG and Molz continued to grow his team, bringing in R. E. Coleman as winemaker in charge of production and cellars, and Ivan F. Kearns as general manager, who also served several terms as president of the Washington Wine Council.

In 1956 AWG sold the "NAWICO building" to a donut company. By 1961 Vic Allison was general manager, and AWG's facilities included "the Pommerelle plant in Seattle, the National Wine Co. plant in Grandview...four grape farms in Yakima Valley [totaling 500 acres], and a several-hundred-acre berry farm on Whidbey Island. Each plant has a capacity of 750,000 gallons of wine a year."[14]

The grapes from their Eastern Washington vineyards were all "shipped to Seattle by stainless steel truck" and AWG invested in state-of-the-art bottling line machinery. A reporter from the *Seattle Times* marveled at its swift and efficient activity: "Bottles are being filled, capped and labeled at a rate of 200 bottles a minute, 2,000 cases a day. All-new bottling equipment has just been installed in the plant—cappers, labelers and filling machines."[15]

HOWARD SOMERS

In 1918—the very year that his father, Charles Somers, bought the old Lambert Evans vineyards out on Stretch Island—Howard Somers was born at Seattle General Hospital. Schooled in Seattle, Somers progressed to the University of Washington, where he earned his bachelor's degree in Chemical Engineering and then received a master's degree from Cornell University. Upon his return from serving in the U.S. Navy during WWII, he partnered with his father, becoming the new winemaker at their St. Charles Winery. After his father's death, the winery was sold and Somers went on to found a business selling equipment and supplies to wineries. Seattle's AWG hired him as a winemaker—a job where he made the first wines under the proprietary name of Ste. Michelle Vineyards in 1967– and he remained aboard when AWG morphed into Ste. Michelle Vintners in 1972. History will remember him for playing a key role in establishing the winery's reputation for making excellent Johannisberg Riesling, the grape that the Washington wine business was built on. Somers became a charter member of the Washington Association of Wine Grape Growers, the American Society of Oenologists, and the Knights of the Vine.

ON THE VINEYARD PATH TO GREATNESS

American Wine Growers was committed to new *vinifera* vineyards: Pinot Noir and Sémillon grapes were planted in 1957, as was Cabernet Sauvignon in 1961. In 1965 AWG planted their first White Riesling in the Yakima Valley at Hahn Hill Vineyards. This variety would go on to define Washington wine for a couple of decades. That same year AWG hired Howard Somers, who would serve as their enologist and was the winemaker of what can be considered the firm's first premium wines.

In 1966 the great wine expert, Leon D. Adams, came touring through the Yakima Valley, tasting wines and visiting the AWG facility in Grandview. While here, Adams suggested to Vic Allison that AWG would be wise to begin making *vinifera* wines on a commercial scale—and that they would benefit by consulting with some knowledgeable people who were active in the robust California wine industry.

A few names were considered, including that of the recently retired André Tchelistcheff, who in 1967 agreed to come north, where he also spent some time tasting an array of wines with Allison at AWG. Tchelistcheff soon developed a theory "that the wines are superior in Washington because the vines go completely dormant in the winter. And when they shut down completely, they come back in the spring and are much more fragrant and powerful."

While Tchelistcheff had second thoughts about the region's grape growing potential, he decided that what was lacking here was something he could bring to the table. He accepted Allison's invitation to serve as a consultant to AWG, advising their capable enologist Howard Somers. He "first directed that the Vinifera vines in the American Wine Growers' vineyards be immediately pruned to reduce the crop and achieve proper sugar-acid balance in the grapes."[16] Conversations about soil types and grape varieties were held with Dr. Clore at the Prosser Experimental Station and new vineyards were planted to Chenin Blanc, Sémillon, and White Riesling, along with classic reds: Cabernet Sauvignon, Grenache, and Pinot Noir. Two years later an array of *vinifera* wines made from Cabernet Sauvignon, Pinot Noir, and Sémillon grapes, as well as a Rosé made from Grenache, were ready to taste.

Hahn Hill
Vineyard manager,
Art Herrmann

The American Wine Growers plant in Seattle was the site of a serious tasting event in the fall of 1969. Attendees included Tchelistcheff, wine author Leon Adams, AWG's Howard Somers, Victor Allison and Ivan Kearns—along with Lloyd Woodburne and Cornelius Peck from the Associated Vintners. Tchelistcheff's "recommendation was that Washington concentrate on Chardonnay, Gewürztraminer, White Riesling, Grenache, and Cabernet Sauvignon; he failed to recognize the real potential of the state for producing the top-quality reds for which it is known today."[17]

ANDRÉ TCHELISTCHEFF

Born and raised in Moscow, Russia, the young André Tchelistcheff served in the anti-communist White Army during the Russian Civil War (1918–1921). After the war he studied agronomy in France and worked in the Department of Viticulture in Paris, where he crossed paths with Georges de Latour in 1937. Latour invited Tchelistcheff to relocate to Napa Valley and work as the enologist (and vice president) at Latour's Beaulieu Vineyards (BV). Tchelistcheff arrived stateside in 1938 and proceeded to establish himself as a leader in the California wine industry.

André Tchelistcheff

Tchelistcheff worked at BV for 35 years, served as a consultant to scores of California wineries (including eventual giants, Robert Mondavi and Louis M. Martini), established his own wine laboratory, and has been credited with creating "the first world-class California cabernet." He "pioneered the cold-fermentation process now widely used in producing white and rosé wines… [and] developed frost-prevention techniques and helped curb vine disease in Napa Valley."[18]

Tchelistcheff's interactions with the nascent Washington wine industry began in 1961, when a group of amateur wine-makers led by Lloyd Woodburne sent their wines to him for feedback. Tchelistcheff "liked all of the wines and declared that the [1960 Grenache-based pink sparkler] was as good as Beaulieu Vineyards." But the significance of his more formal contributions as a consultant to Seattle's American Wine Growers in 1967—and on through their morphing into Ste. Michelle, and up through 1990—cannot be over-stated. Interestingly, the man who the *San Francisco Chronicle* noted as "the dean of American winemakers" never cared much about wealth, just knowl-edge and wine, saying once: "Money is the dust of life. I don't have a wine cellar, I don't have a vineyard, I don't have nothing. I only have my head."[19]

Left to right: Walter Clore, Tchelistcheff, and Leon Adams

THE DEBUT OF STE. MICHELLE

On August 1, 1969, AWG unveiled the commercial debut of their *vinifera* wines hailing from the 1967 and 1968 harvests (which yielded a total of 15,000 gallons of Cabernet Sauvignon, Grenache Rosé, Pinot Noir, and Sémillon-Blanc). AWG also hit the marketplace under a new brand: Ste. Michelle Vineyards. The French name was selected as a nod to the Old World. Several names of European flavor were considered, first informally at a dinner party that included Vic Allison, Joe Molz, and others, then later at a company meeting. Legend has it that Molz's daughter, who had recently returned from a European trip where she'd been overwhelmed by the beauty of Mont Saint-Michel island just off the Normandy Coast, favored the name "Sainte Michelle."

Considering that almost 90 percent of Washington wine at that time was still fruit based or fortified, the very idea of presenting a European-style wine label represented cutting-edge thinking. Introduced to the California market, the initial response from the San Francisco Sampling Club was inspiring. They deemed the wine as one that was "challenging the quality supremacy of California varietal wines."[20]

Ste. Michelle Vineyards debuts, 1969

Meanwhile, AWG was still based out of the old Pommerelle building on E. Marginal Way S., whose bleak location the *Seattle Times* once colorfully described as being "in the middle of the southern industrial flats between the gray of the Duwamish [River], the brown of Boeing and the baked enamel of Kenworth trucks." The setting was given further ambience from overhead: "the northern-approach landing pattern at Sea-Tac [International Airport] thunders a few feet over stainless steel tanks of white wine and the oak and redwood vats of claret. Nobody would mistake it for a Burgundian chalet; clearly it is not a Rhine castle."[21]

True, but that was about to change with the development of the grand Chateau Ste. Michelle winery estate property nestled in the rustic wilds of Woodinville, Washington.

Chapter Three

A BUDDING BUSINESS

STE. MICHELLE WINES

The American wine industry experienced significant change as the turbulent decade of the 1960s drew to a close. This was primarily due to a shift in marketplace demand. Increasing affluence and a related rise in awareness about finer wines was causing consumer tastes to trend toward the more elegant and lighter *vitis vinifera*-based dry table wines from California, whose industry had long dominated the American marketplace.

In the Pacific Northwest, this upheaval was particularly pronounced in the wake of major changes in Washington State's liquor laws. Luckily, Chateau Ste. Michelle would be perfectly poised to make the most of the coming wine revolution, and in doing so would soon become *the* preeminent symbol of the Washington wine industry.

Since 1935 Washington law had favored the distribution of Washington wines over California wines. The law was not without controversy and a 1969 lawsuit from California brought new scrutiny to the issue. The handful of active wineries in Washington that had effectively grown a bit dependent on the embargo now fumed that changes in the law would endanger their business model. Specifically, they risked losing their control of shelf space in privately owned grocery stores. On the other hand, most of the wine grapes grown in Washington at the time were Concord grapes, shipped south to California for use in sweet wine production. It was unclear what the effects of deregulation would be.

A DISTINCTIVE VARIETAL TABLE WINE

Ste. Michelle Vineyards®

Washington State

Chenin Blanc

Produced from Chenin Blanc Grapes grown in the Yakima Valley

PRODUCED AND BOTTLED BY

Ste. Michelle Vineyards

SEATTLE, WASHINGTON

ALCOHOL 12% BY VOLUME

Chenin Blanc label, circa 1974

Among the experts called to testify at the legislative hearings were Dr. Walter Clore and Dr. Charles "Chas" Nagel. "Clore told the lawmakers that he had been "researching the potential of 'the *vinifera* type of grape. This is the European type of grape…We have been working since 1937, at least I have, on grape varieties and grape problems in the Yakima Valley.'"[22]

Clore's research indicated that Washington growers had every reason to think they could compete vigorously with California in the newly burgeoning fine wine market. Clore pointed out that Washington was on the same latitude as the fine wine growing regions of Europe; that Washington had a longer growing season, with more hours of more intense sunlight; and that Washington's grape growing regions were not plagued with the insects and diseases California had. Clore's colleague, Dr. Nagel, who had organized one of his tasting panels that rated about 50 local wines, added further to the argument. "When he was asked how Washington wines compared with wines grown and made elsewhere, Nagel replied, 'In my opinion, quite favorably with certain varieties of any produced in the world, according to our taste panel.'"[23]

THE CALIFORNIA WINE BILL

The two scientists' testimony was quite persuasive and the legislature passed the California Wine Bill. Sales of California wines increased in Washington and, in the short run, local wineries were under great pressure. This new strain was caused in part by the bill's ruling that all wines would be taxed at 26 percent, instead of the former 15 percent rate. The *Seattle Times* editorialized: "Wine consumers in Washington now have a better selection of wines as a result of the new distribution system, but the improvement unfortunately is at their expense."

AWG Winery, Seattle

Seattle's AWG was among those suddenly feeling the pressure of having good quality out-of-state wines competing for shelf space in area stores. Records reveal that in 1970, local wineries had produced 1,871,758 gallons of wine, but by 1975 that figure had fallen to 906,565. However, the public's tastes were clearly evolving and there would be no turning back.

Fortunately, AWG had already thought ahead and their new Ste. Michelle brand proudly featured *vinifera*-based wines. Still, the transition was not easy. General Manager Vic Allison was a bit dismayed that sales weren't going as well as hoped when he received a phone call from Sacramento. On the other end of the line was Charles Finkel, a former sales ace from the New York-based importer and distributor, Monsieur Henri Wines, who had gone on to form his own distributorship, Bon-Vin.

Finkel informed Allison that he had just sampled some of the 1967 Ste. Michelle wines, loved them, and wanted to be the winery's national sales agent. A meeting was soon held in Seattle, and Finkel ended up walking away with a contract naming Bon-Vin as AWG's exclusive new agent (in every state except Washington and

Charles and Rose Ann Finkel, circa 1974

Oregon, which AWG wanted to retain). Allotted 3,000 cases that first year, Finkel and company apparently had no problem moving the product, and within five years they were being allotted 25,000 cases to sell. By 1974 Finkel was brought aboard as the winery's director of sales (he also later served as VP of marketing).

These first Ste. Michelle wines were merely spearheading the still-long road ahead to create a new national awareness about the potential quality of Washington wine. But an ever-growing segment of the local population had their interest piqued by all the attention being paid to the topic, and serious progress lay just ahead.

Chapter Four

IN BLOOM

STE. MICHELLE VINTNERS, INC.

W ashington wines had been capturing the attention of several key figures who would prove to play critical roles in the coming revolution in the industry. One was journalist Stan Reed, who had been publishing a series of feature articles on various aspects of the business since 1969 in the *Seattle Post-Intelligencer.* Another was one of his faithful readers, Wallace "Wally" E. Opdycke, a 32-year-old investment portfolio manager at Seattle's Safeco Insurance Company who had just received his MBA degree from the University of Washington. Opdycke was transfixed by Reed's articles about the nascent Washington wine scene. As someone who had already worked in San Francisco and had enjoyed visiting Napa Valley wineries, he found the potential for an expanded wine industry in Washington quite intriguing. "Three things hit me," recalled Opdycke. "The quality of the grapes, the yield per acre, which was higher than, say, Napa, and the cost of land, which was lower."[24]

After a phone conversation with Dr. Walter Clore about the true potential for growing high quality grapes in the region, Opdycke became further intrigued. "While at work at Safeco one day, I'd gone out for a cup of coffee and came back and my secretary said, 'There's somebody here to see you.' And by gosh, it was Dr. Clore! I couldn't believe it. We talked some more and hit it off. He told me 'We really need some more people like you.'" Dr. Clore gave Opdycke several leads, organizing several meetings with experts in the lower Yakima Valley and encouraging Opdycke to get involved. Opdycke decided that the timing was right and when he asked Clore if he would help, the Father of Washington Wine said, "Absolutely."

In 1970 Opdycke began touring Eastern Washington grape country, checking out AWG's vineyards and even scouting William Bridgman's old Upland Winery facility. He felt that starting totally from scratch was too risky and preferred to buy into the business. "I did a little research," he recalled, "And found out that American Wine Growers was the only operating winery outside of Associated Vintners at that point. Everybody else was out of business or close to being out of business. So that was the impetus for me."[25]

He also surmised that AWG was ailing in the wake of the overturning of the protectionist laws back in 1969. But beyond all that, Opdycke had tried AWG's Ste. Michelle Cabernet and Pinot Noir and just *knew* they could be improved. So Opdycke requested a meeting with Joe Molz, where he would learn that the now-aging owners of the winery were, in fact, ready to sell.

Opdycke assembled a group of Seattle-based investors (including attorney Mike Garvey, along with Kirby Cramer and Don Nielsen) who put together a business plan, pooled their resources, and successfully acquired AWG in 1972. The deal covered the company's valuable wine-production license, wine brands, enology equipment, and properties (including the company's multiple vineyards, which were maturing nicely). On May 1, 1973, the company was officially recast as Ste. Michelle Vintners, Inc. Opdycke, the newly minted winery president, told the *Seattle Times* that "within 10 to 15 years, Washington could be second only to California in grape and wine production."

Ripening grapes at Cold Creek

Top: Wally Opdyke, circa 1976

From left: Mike Garvey, Joe Molz, and Wally Opdyke, circa 1972

One of the new company's first moves was to invest in the planting of their Cold Creek Vineyard, a 500-acre plot, as originally recommended by Dr. Clore. In so doing, they doubled the total acreage of vines in the state. Meanwhile, André Tchelistcheff continued advising the winery through the transition and advocated employing a secondary malolactic fermentation in their red wines.

COLD CREEK VINEYARD

In 1973 the newly incorporated Ste. Michelle Vintners took the bold step of acquiring a large plot of desolate, sun-drenched land just north of the Yakima Valley town of Sunnyside. Comprised of hayfields and a small seasonal creek, the land had a bit of Old West flavor to it. In the late 1850s it had been used by cattle baron Ben Snipes to graze his herds before they were driven to market via Canada's Okanogan Valley. After the Homestead Act of 1862, farmers settled the land, founded a nursery, and grew crops using dry-land farming and water pumped from artesian wells, which were more dependable than the creek.

A century after the Homestead Act, the physical attributes of the site caught the eye of WSU researcher Dr. Walter Clore and he recommended it to Ste. Michelle, resulting in the highly treasured Cold Creek Vineyard, one of the company's crown jewels. Essentially a bowl accessed via a gap in the Rattlesnake Hills just below the Columbia River, the vineyard features Warden silt loam and associated soils. At an elevation of 600–1,000 feet above sea level and an orientation with a gentle (3%–5%) south-facing slope away from the river, the land was potentially highly suited to grapes.

Cold Creek Vineyard

Stan Bowman,
Equipment Foreman
at Cold Creek, 1976

Planted as a massive 500-acre plot in the summer of 1973, the vineyard became a topic of much discussion in surrounding agricultural communities. No one had seen anything like it attempted in such a hot and dry (five inches of rain per year) location. But Clore's experiments and testing had indicated it would be an excellent grape growing site—one known today as being among the very best in the Columbia Valley AVA. Initially "almost every varietal popular at the time was planted at Cold Creek," Ste. Michelle's VP of Vineyards Kevin Corliss, recalls. "However, four decades of experience and research has led to replacing rootstock with varieties that thrive in the hot, stressed conditions of this remote area." Today Cold Creek Vineyard is an 811-acre site whose vines produce a remarkable number of highly esteemed wines. "We make Cold Creek Vineyard Chardonnay, Riesling, Cabernet Sauvignon, Merlot, and Syrah and they are all intense, concentrated expressions of the varietals," says Chateau Ste. Michelle Head Winemaker Bob Bertheau. And because of their structure, "Cold Creek wines have great aging potential. Our Cold Creek Cabernet can age for decades. But if you can't wait that long, we make the wine so you can enjoy it now, too."

Cold Creek's unique terroir, along with Ste. Michelle's commitment to research and innovation at the vineyard, has won these wines critical acclaim. In addition, the site—which is farmed using sustainable, environmentally safe, and socially acceptable vineyard management practices, has earned accolades for being the largest LIVE and Salmon Safe certified site in Washington.

Cold Creek row
ID marker

Les Fleming at Cold Creek, 1973

This is a biological process in which a bacterial fermentation causes a softening of the wine, while giving the juice greater complexity. In 1974 with the addition of the UC Davis–trained winemaker Joel Klein to their team, Ste. Michelle achieved its first complete malolactic fermentation. It was an important step forward, demonstrating the winery's commitment to push the quality of its wines to the next level.

In 1974 Ste. Michelle's 1972 White Riesling became the very first Pacific Northwest wine to win a major tasting competition. The *Los Angeles Times* had assembled a tasting panel of seven experts that was led by the prominent wine writer Robert Lawrence Balzer and included California winemakers Robert Mondavi and André Tchelistcheff. They rounded up 19 Riesling wines from Germany and California and, probably for diversity, included one Washington wine.

When the blind tasting was concluded and the Ste. Michelle wine was revealed as top ranked, the grinning was happening up in Seattle. As so many of the other competitors were top wines from prestigious wineries, this surprise verdict must have been painful for some folks. "As a final blow, the Ste. Michelle was the least expensive of all the wines, proving once again that you can't judge a wine by its price or label."[26] The winery was suddenly catapulted into the national spotlight. Washington's branding as the home of high quality Riesling had begun. It was a deserved reputation that would carry forth for decades—and one that soon saw Ste. Michelle's 1973 Semillon being served during a formal dinner at President Gerald R. Ford's White House.

Opdyke and Finkel lead a distributor tour at Cold Creek, 1977

Ste. Michelle Vintners' management team, which still included Vic Allison (now as VP and GM), pressed forward on many fronts. After first considering hiring California's estimable Mike Grgich—a talented protégé of André Tchelistcheff—the winery instead named Joel Klein their new winemaker in 1974. Klein had studied chemical engineering at the Polytechnic Institute of Brooklyn, and then, intrigued by wine, he moved west to study at UC Davis. The university's Department of Viticulture and Enology, established in 1935, was the leading wine education center in the United States. Klein's entrée into the wine industry was as the designer of California's Geyser Peak Winery. But after joining the Ste. Michelle team, he contributed greatly throughout the company's start-up phase before leading their winemaking up through 1982.

On a path to greater success, the owners began seeking out an infusion of additional capital to aid in their expansion plans. In February 1974 Wally Opdycke hammered out a deal with the Greenwich, Connecticut, based U.S. Tobacco Co. (UST)—makers of the *Skoal* and *Copenhagen* brands of smokeless tobacco products—which was looking to diversify. That infusion of capital made Ste. Michelle Vintners the big driver of the Washington wine business. It also greatly accelerated the winery's ability to become a major player in the wine world. A year later they were producing 30,000 cases a year, distributing across thirty states—and Ste. Michelle Vintners harvested its first Chardonnay grapes.

In 1975 another significant milestone was just around the corner. The catalyst was the Port of Seattle's announcement that their operations required the acquisition of the old Pommerelle headquarters on East Marginal Way.

AWG (Pommerelle) Winery, Seattle

MODERN FACILITIES

large spotless plant

The Pommerelle plant at 9417 East Marginal Way, Seattle, is one of the largest and most modern wineries in the State. From the stainless steel filters to the huge storage tanks of 500,000 gallons capacity, complete facilities are available for crushing, fermenting, distilling, storing, bottling and shipping grape, berry and kosher wines of the finest quality. Also on the premises is a Government bonded warehouse. It pays to sell the leader.

Chapter Five

FULL FLOWER

CHATEAU STE. MICHELLE

The leadership of Ste. Michelle Vintners had already begun scouting around for a location to construct a major new winery. They considered placing it in the heart of the vineyard country of Eastern Washington—in either Yakima or Sunnyside.

But in 1973 when Wally Opdycke stumbled across an 87-acre plot of land (currently 105 acres) situated just south of the tiny rural town of Woodinville, Washington, he just knew he had found the right spot. Conveniently located 15 miles northeast of the population center of Seattle, the historic Hollywood Farm property had been developed by Northwest timber baron Frederick Stimson. That history, along with the pastoral setting, was perfect for a project that Ste. Michelle Vintners had in mind.

Ste. Michelle Vintners acquired the farm from the MacBride family for $230,000 and began to reimagine the future of their enterprise—one they felt should reflect the noble grandeur of the European wine tradition. "We wanted to build it to look like an old French chateau," Opdycke recalled. And along with that image upgrade, "We decided to change the name from Ste. Michelle Vintners to Chateau Ste. Michelle."[27]

FREDERICK STIMSON AND
THE HOLLYWOOD FARM

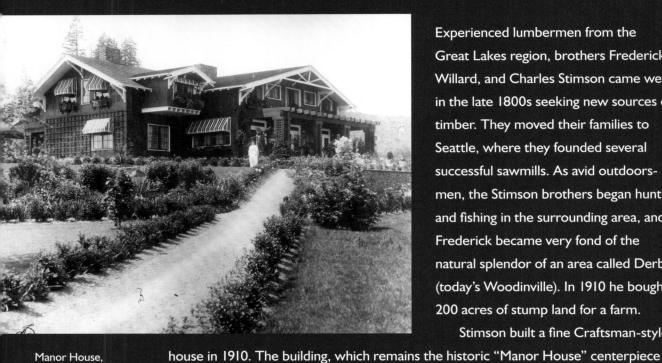

Manor House,
circa 1915

Experienced lumbermen from the Great Lakes region, brothers Frederick, Willard, and Charles Stimson came west in the late 1800s seeking new sources of timber. They moved their families to Seattle, where they founded several successful sawmills. As avid outdoorsmen, the Stimson brothers began hunting and fishing in the surrounding area, and Frederick became very fond of the natural splendor of an area called Derby (today's Woodinville). In 1910 he bought 200 acres of stump land for a farm.

Stimson built a fine Craftsman-style house in 1910. The building, which remains the historic "Manor House" centerpiece of the property today, included six bedrooms, four rooms for domestics' quarters, four river rock fireplaces, and a cozy sunroom. Set upon a hillock just above his fields along the Sammamish River, the house served Stimson as a weekend getaway for his family and as a hunting retreat for him and his friends.

Built adjacent to the house was a large carriage house—big enough to shelter his growing fleet of automobiles, which included an early electric car. High-tech innovations interested Stimson, and he developed a state-of-the-art dairy operation that boasted its own power plant for the gigantic new barns. Stimson also financed a private railroad spur built across the now 600-acre property, so that the barns could be linked directly with the Woodinville-to-Redmond branch of the Great Northern Railway line that ran between Snohomish in the north and Renton in the south. This was much more efficient than shipping his farm products into Seattle by truck.

Surrounding the house were spectacular grounds that featured a gated and well-lit paved driveway, lighted tennis courts, a laundry, private trout ponds, many beautiful trees, and tastefully designed gardens. It is believed that Stimson's wife, Nellie, a plant

Hollywood booklet,
circa 1927

Milking time at
Hollywood

52

enthusiast, directed the development of the gardens. The Stimsons also planted over 200 holly trees lining Stimson Lane, the road that led up to the house. The property came to be called Hollywood Farm as a nod to those trees—but quite possibly also as a means of creating a little sheen of glamour over the reality of raising pigs and operating a dairy with 300 head of pure-bred Holsteins.

In 1913 Stimson took on a partner, Mort E. Atkinson, who built up a 17-acre chicken farm called Hollywood Poultry Farm, which grew to 47 acres with annual revenue over $100,000. Atkinson proved to be a remarkably successful chicken breeder. In the 1920s his unique strain of "Hollywood" birds gained nationwide fame through contests, achieving world-record-setting status as prolific egg-layers, and his most prized hen, Lady Hollywood, became a star unto her own.

The dairy was driven by state-of-the-art technology and business practices. The Stimsons "created an innovative, modern dairy that employed scientific methods of management, stringent quality controls, and direct marketing techniques, allowing customers to afford the best, most pure milk."[28] Stimson's decision to sell his farm's products directly to customers in 1916

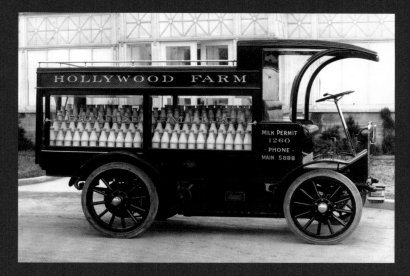

Hollywood Farm milk delivery truck, 1913

led him to halt his delivery service and open the Hollywood Farm City Store. Situated on Westlake Avenue in downtown Seattle, the store had a sit-down lunch counter, which also served as an ice cream parlor and soda fountain.

Following that success, Nellie opened her own Hollywood Gardens floral shop in downtown Seattle where she sold the carnations, roses, and orchids raised by staff gardeners in nine greenhouses built on the Hollywood Farm property. In 1918, when Stimson's doctor advised him that country living might be better for his health, the couple and their three children moved to the estate for good. After Stimson's early death in 1921, Nellie and her son Harold kept the farm operation running with the assistance of their farm manager, Mr. Peters. But by 1931 they were ready to sell.

Portions of the farm were leased out to other operations for a period—including a dairy run by the Alex and Fanny Sender family—but it eventually fell into serious disrepair. By the early 1940s Philip and Frances MacBride bought the farm and began restoring it. Like Nellie before her, Frances loved plants. She reworked the overgrown gardens, planting fruit trees, a vegetable garden, and even some of the exotic imported tree specimens still enjoyed by visitors today. After Frances MacBride passed away in 1972, the family sold the old Hollywood Farm to Ste. Michelle Vintners.

Previous Pages:

Hollywood Farm

Estate, from

Hollywood Hill

GROUNDBREAKING CHANGES

On September 24, 1975, a formal groundbreaking ceremony was held at the site of what would eventually become famous as the Chateau Ste. Michelle winery. Among the most prominent attendees was Governor Daniel J. Evans, who gamely wielded a spade to help plant a symbolic grapevine on the grounds. The ambitious redevelopment of the Stimson property required a $6 million expenditure, but it included the construction of a stunning 150,000-square-foot French-style chateau. The magnificent building was designed by Paul Brenna of the Chester L. Lindsay & Associates architectural firm with structural engineering by Kelly, Pittelko, Fritz & Forssen and construction by the Howard S. Wright Construction Company.

The Chateau under

construction, 1976

The expansive grounds with their countless mature trees would also be improved. As the *Seattle Times* noted: "The 600-foot-long new building will have space for fermenting, aging, bottling, warehousing, crushing and pressing. Administrative offices and a visitor center and wine-tasting room will be near the main entrance to the two-story chateau." The winery's president, Wally Opdycke, "predicts the winery will be the most modern in America."[29]

One person who attended the groundbreaking event would, a year later, become one of Chateau Ste. Michelle's most consequential staff hirings. A young Seattleite with an interest in wine and a bachelor of science degree from the University of

Bob Betz

Washington, Bob Betz had recently spent a full year in Europe immersing himself in wine culture, visiting chateaux, harvesting grapes, and even dabbling in winemaking in the Loire Valley. Upon his return to Seattle, Betz called Charles Finkel at Chateau Ste. Michelle and said, "'Hi! I'm back!' And Charles said: 'Who are you?' And I told him my story and he said: 'Well, thanks for calling. We'll call you back when we want to talk to you.' And, bless him—it was about ten months later and he called and said: 'We'd like to talk to you.'" Betz made a great impression at the winery, in part because "there weren't a lot of people in town at that time with first-hand knowledge of other vineyard regions. And, I had a science background. So I could speak the language somewhat. Wine was not a mystery to me. And I think one of the best things was: I had a global perspective. I had been exposed to the industry leaders at the time."

Betz began work on January 1, 1976. "I started down at the Marginal Way site as director of public relations. I was then part of the transition team that moved to Woodinville. In August of 1976 we moved all the offices, all the winemaking equipment, and had it all in place for the harvest of '76." His specific tasks were a challenge. "A lot of what I did early on was new. They asked me to write a press release about the move and I had to look up the words 'press release.'"

THE GRAND OPENING

After completing the transformation of the Hollywood Farm property—and issuing a press release or two—the company held grand opening events in September of 1976. The Chateau threw open its doors to 2,000 invited guests who were treated to wine and Pacific Northwest appetizers like smoked salmon, clams, and oysters while enjoying a string quartet, strolling the park-like grounds, and touring the winery. Even the specially produced 1975 White Riesling wine bottles showed off their new name: *Chateau* Ste. Michelle.

1975 Chateau label debuts, 1976

"With a sip of this rich and fragrant wine each guest quietly understood the why of the occasion."[30] The back labels of these new Chateau Ste. Michelle wine bottles featured a memorable graphic design element intended to intrigue and educate people about the "why" behind the effort to grow *vinifera* grapes in Washington: location and terroir. It was a simplified global map showing that this agricultural zone was aligned with the exact same latitude as that of two exceptional wine regions in France: Burgundy and Bordeaux.

The grand Chateau would come to serve as a very visible public nexus for the Washington wine scene. Original estimates for the number of expected visitors was a hopeful 40,000 guests per year. It was a nice surprise when over 250,000 visitors walked through the doors, even in those early years.

GETTING DOWN TO BUSINESS

With Chateau Ste. Michelle's debut complete, it was time to get down to business and focus on achieving the company's goal of increasing wine production in the new winery to 100,000 cases per year. To that end, the company harvested its first Merlot

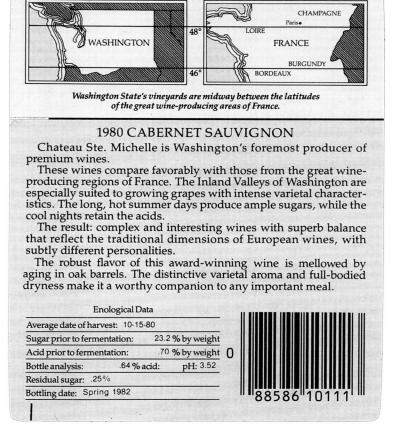

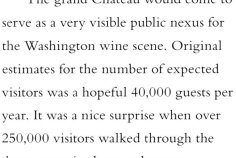

Washington State's vineyards are midway between the latitudes of the great wine-producing areas of France.

1980 CABERNET SAUVIGNON

Chateau Ste. Michelle is Washington's foremost producer of premium wines.

These wines compare favorably with those from the great wine-producing regions of France. The Inland Valleys of Washington are especially suited to growing grapes with intense varietal characteristics. The long, hot summer days produce ample sugars, while the cool nights retain the acids.

The result: complex and interesting wines with superb balance that reflect the traditional dimensions of European wines, with subtly different personalities.

The robust flavor of this award-winning wine is mellowed by aging in oak barrels. The distinctive varietal aroma and full-bodied dryness make it a worthy companion to any important meal.

Enological Data

Average date of harvest:	10-15-80	
Sugar prior to fermentation:	23.2 % by weight	
Acid prior to fermentation:	.70 % by weight	
Bottle analysis:	.64 % acid:	pH: 3.52
Residual sugar:	.25%	
Bottling date:	Spring 1982	

88586 10111

Group at winery, Grandview, including Vic Allison, Dorothy Tchelistcheff, Wally Opdycke, Walt Clore, and André Tchelistcheff

grapes, which would soon spark a new consumer trend. Among the initial executive staff members were Bill McKelvey in finance and old-school wine-sales pro, Bill Stuht, who within a decade rose to become VP of international sales and marketing.

After the excitement around opening the new winery, Chateau Ste. Michelle took a realistic appraisal of the winery's first wines and decided there was clearly room to improve, both in reducing acidity and in achieving overall balance. Utilizing grapes

Washington & France share wine-producing latitudes, as this 1980 label describes.

from young vines is a common issue for young wineries, but usually one that can be overcome with a few more vintages under their belts. "For Washington, and for Chateau Ste. Michelle, consistent success with red wine was long in coming, but by the late '70s, much had been learned about growing grapes and making the wine."[31] Up until the late 1970s, the company's Cabernet Sauvignon and Merlot wines had been aged in American oak barrels, which "imparted a strong flavor into the young red wines." But in 1978 the winery released a reserve Cabernet that had been aged in French oak.[32] The upgrade in quality was clear, and by 1981 the winery even started using French oak for some of its standard Cabernet and Merlot wines, significantly improving those wines as well.

In 1977 a gifted young enologist, Kay Simon, joined the team. The year prior she had graduated from UC Davis and had worked a couple of harvest seasons with California's San Joaquin Valley-based United Vintners. During a brief visit to the

Pacific Northwest, she was given a few bottles of Chateau Ste. Michelle's Riesling and was intrigued enough to take a tour of the winery. Her tour guide quickly recognized her expertise after she asked a few technically astute questions and introduced Simon to then Head Winemaker Joel Klein. Klein mentioned that they just happened to have an assistant winemaker position open. Simon was hired and by 1978 she was overseeing the making of the winery's first Cold Creek Vineyard Cabernet Sauvignon.

"It was really a fun time to be employed by them," Simon recalls. "They had all this backing money. 'You want a new press? Go buy one.' 'You need a hundred new barrels? Go buy them.' There was plenty of cash to do what you thought would work and that made it exciting. The Woodinville-based executives were by-and-large business guys, not wine industry guys. So, there was a lot of responsibility given to young people—many of us who had come up from California with the technical degrees that were lacking and not yet offered in Washington State. We were given—in our early-to-mid-twenties—a lot of leeway. That made it fun and exciting but also a little daunting."

That same year Dr. Wade Wolfe, a viticulturist with a degree from UC Davis, was recruited by Chateau Ste. Michelle. Wolfe eventually served as head viticulturist, and he and Dr. Walter Clore collaborated on the proposal to establish the Columbia Valley AVA.

Cabernet bottles show design evolution of labels, 1967-2003

Allen Shoup, 1980

In the winter of 1978 an early November freeze occurred. Some Johannisberg Riesling grapes, having been left on the vine during the freeze, resulted in the production of the winery's first "Ice Wine." It also resulted in the destruction of many of the vines at Cold Creek Vineyard. The vineyard was replanted and then expanded to include Cabernet (344 acres), Riesling (161 acres), Chardonnay (92 acres), Merlot (83 acres), and Muscat Canelli (37 acres).

With this growth, Chateau Ste. Michelle sought out a professional to manage their marketing efforts and in 1980 hired Allen Shoup. Shoup brought with him high-level branding experience as a marketing manager with Ernest & Julio Gallo's California wine empire. One of his initial tasks was to begin building a sales force that could represent the company nationally, and eventually on an international basis.

GOLD MEDALS AND BIG CHANGES

In November of 1982 Bob Betz got a call from Milan, Italy, where the *Sesto Concorso Enologico Internazionale* wine competition is held every other vintage year. Chateau Ste. Michelle had submitted six of their finest wines to face off against 450 others from around the globe. The judging was overseen by agents of the Italian Ministry of Agriculture and taken very seriously by the worldwide wine industry.

Betz could not believe what he was hearing. "'Five of your wines won!" a judge reported in thick, static-filled Italian. 'Won what?' asked [Betz]. 'First prizes! Gold Medals! Five of them!' The awards not only honored Chateau Ste. Michelle's accomplishments; they also helped confirm Washington's international status as a producer of premium *vinifera* wines."[33]

Cheryl Barber-Jones, 1985

In 1983—the year that the Yakima Valley was formally established as Washington's first AVA—Chateau Ste. Michelle produced an astounding 1.8 million gallons of wine, making it America's second largest premium wine producer. There were leadership changes as well. Wally Opdycke retired as president and was briefly replaced by Hank Schones, a former executive with New York's Monsieur Henri Wines. In addition, Peter Bachman (a graduate of California Polytechnic and former employee at California's Almaden Winery and Monterey Vineyard) was hired as director of winery operations, and Cheryl Barber, who started with Ste. Michelle in 1976 as a lab technician, was promoted to head winemaker. Looking toward future growth, Chateau Ste. Michelle began planting the Horse Heaven Vineyard.

HORSE HEAVEN VINEYARD

The origins of the name of the Horse Heaven Hills AVA remain shrouded in the mists of time. Some sources attribute it to cattleman Ben Snipes, who in 1856 was impressed by this long range of rolling hills which stretch westward from the Columbia River, and between the Yakima River and the Wallula Gap in south-central Washington. Others cite another local pioneer settler, James G. Kinney, who reportedly saw the roaming bands of wild horses in the area and exclaimed, "This is surely a horse heaven!"

Just as its proximity to the Columbia River made this hot area attractive to wild horses down through millennia, so too does the majestic river help make it beneficial to grape growing. The landscape's physical profile of south-facing slopes helps moderate temperatures with the river current stirring the summer heat. Conversely, the winter's heavy cold air is drained away along those same slopes. Chateau Ste. Michelle's 469-acre vineyard is planted in soil comprised of silty loam and sand over a rocky volcanic base of fractured basalt. First planted to Chenin Blanc and Sauvignon Blanc in 1983, low rainfall and this free-draining soil allow Chateau Ste. Michelle to control drip-irrigation levels, keeping the grapevines from becoming overly aggressive. This tempered vine vigor helps delay harvest, providing a long hang time for clusters and uniform ripening. The result is dependably crisp, graceful, seamless wines.

Horse Heaven Vineyard

Chapter Six

GROWING UP

CULTIVATING A REPUTATION

The mid-1980s brought new leadership during a dynamic era in Chateau Ste. Michelle's history. Allen Shoup, who came to the company in 1980 with strong ties to California wine luminaries like Ernest Gallo and Robert Mondavi, had worked his way up the ranks and took over as president and CEO in 1984. That same year, Bob Betz was elevated to VP of communications and Ted Baseler was brought on board as director of marketing.

Baseler had been an account executive with Cole & Weber Advertising, the leading ad agency in the Pacific Northwest at the time. A local kid with a marketing degree from Washington State University and a master's degree from Northwestern, Baseler worked for the J. Walter Thompson Advertising agency in Chicago for four years before returning to Seattle. Upon his return he discovered that the region's fine-wine industry had taken off while he was away—and Chateau Ste. Michelle was one of his newly assigned Cole & Weber clients.

Ted Baseler, circa 1978

"I was an account guy," Baseler recently recalled, "and I had a real passion for wine. Even though there was very little ad revenue, I loved coming out to the Chateau and chatting with the marketing staff and talking to the winemakers. I did that for a couple years, then when Allen Shoup was promoted to president, he said: 'How would you like my old job?'" Baseler accepted his offer. "We were very eager that year because we were supposed to turn the company's first profit. And we were all excited that we'd make some money and all the books would close that year. And then, four months after I arrived, it was announced that we were going to *lose* $3 million. Unexpectedly. And I thought: "Well, *this* is going to be a short-term gig! I'm not going to be around *here* very long!"

The opening of Chateau Ste. Michelle was big news locally.

The team certainly had their work cut out for them. Although the 1980s saw a growing public interest in fine wines—especially varieties like Merlot, which Chateau Ste. Michelle had invested heavily in—the regional industry still faced uphill marketing battles. The central problem was a lack of national and global public awareness. "Nobody even knew that Washington made wine," Shoup explained. One of the challenges of marketing Washington wines outside the state was to "keep people from laughing when we told them we grow grapes in Washington."[34]

"We'd go to the East Coast," Baseler agreed, "and people would snicker when you said 'Washington wine.'"[35] Bob Betz recalls a telling incident that revealed the lack of a public profile for wine from this state. "In 1978 or '79 I was doing a Washington wine presentation in Orlando, Florida, for a wine club—smart people. We had Washington wines on the table that we were tasting. I had slides of Washington vineyards projecting on the wall. I had talked 30 or 45 minutes about Washington wine. And almost the first question asked was: 'Which side of the Potomac River do you grow your grapes on?' That was the biggest challenge that we faced."

One problem, according to Baseler, was lack of salespeople, which kept most of the winery's market in Washington State. "We had to build a sales force that could take us to fifty states." The other dilemma, Baseler recalled, was the culture clash between the quest for the perfect wine and the need to make a profit. "We had fine wine people who could wax on forever about the great wines of the world on one hand, and...we had the reality...that we've got to make a profit on the other." Baseler had an analytical approach to business and knew the winery needed to increase sales. "Promoting, advertising, and developing a national footprint for our wines really helped."

MARTHA SAYS: "IT'S A GOOD THING"

Shoup, Baseler, and Betz shared the imperative to drive wine sales by creating publicity and they took on the task with gusto. In May of 1984 Chateau Ste. Michelle hosted a press conference in New York City, using the opportunity to pour its 1983 Johannisberg Riesling and 1978 Cabernet. Shoup announced that the winery was committing $5 million toward the Statue of Liberty-Ellis Island Foundation's post-Bicentennial restoration effort.

Quizzed about why they were supporting that particular project, Shoup explained: "We looked at a lot of alternatives for worthy causes, and we decided early on that we wanted it to be not only something meaningful in and of itself, but also something that had a relationship with the winery and fine wines. We leapt at the chance to contribute because we recognized that most of the European immigrants came through Ellis Island." The immigrants, he added, "brought to this country their appreciation for fine wines and foods. [T]he wines are designed to celebrate...[but it] is bigger than a statue and a building...It has to do with the very spirit of freedom in this country. No state better exemplifies that spirit than we do here. We are a state of pioneers and free thinkers."[36]

Chateau Ste. Michelle's Johannisberg Riesling label

That, and because "Ste. Michelle doesn't have a lot of recognition east of the Mississippi." A *Seattle Times* reporter added: "This is calculated to be a bold stroke which will provide more favorable attention than would $5 million of national advertising."[37] "It's not altruism in its purest form, but it's altruism in its most honest form. Everybody benefits."[38] Lady Liberty certainly did, and so did the winery.

The donation was only part of the plan. "One of my first charges," Baseler recalled, "was to hire a book designer and create a book for the Statue of Liberty" project. As design director for the project, he dove right in, interviewing reps from several design firms, including a fellow named Andy Stewart from New York publisher Stewart, Tabori & Chang. "Stewart came out and drew pages of what this book called *Tastes of Liberty* should be about. And he said: 'We'll get historic photos; we will

Tastes of Liberty

have beautiful photography that will reveal these recipes; and we'll tell about how these immigrants came through Ellis Island by the Statue of Liberty—and that they brought their most precious family assets: their family recipes.' It was brilliant."

Bob Betz would serve as the book's editor, hiring a stable of wine writers to pen particular chapters. Amazingly enough, upon publication in 1985, *Tastes of Liberty: A Celebration of our Great Ethnic Cooking* was an instant hit. As it happened, when Andy Stewart introduced Baseler to his wife, the television hostess Martha Stewart, Baseler recalled Martha's comment: "I keep looking at that latitude map on the back label [of the Ste. Michelle wine bottles] and [thinking] about Washington being at the same latitude as Bordeaux. I really believe that there is something to that. Because your wines taste much more European than Californian." Martha's comments were inspirational for Chateau Ste. Michelle's efforts to grow their national reputation.

At various times on her TV show, Martha Stewart would bring out Chateau Ste. Michelle wine and talk about how good it was. The book became a *New York Times* best seller and went on to sell a quarter of a million copies.

RIVER RIDGE WINERY

Grand Opening of River Ridge, 1983, with Chateau Ste. Michelle President Hank Schones (left) and Leon Adams

Less than a decade after opening the Chateau, the company had already outgrown its winemaking capacity. The answer to the problem was building a large sister winery in Eastern Washington, overlooking the Columbia River near the town of Paterson. This was the site of the recently planted 2,000-acre vineyard that Wally Opdycke had impressed Allen Shoup with on their 1980 tour.

In June of 1983 the $26 million Chateau Ste. Michelle River Ridge winery and visitor center opened in an enormous new space nearly three times the size of the Chateau in Woodinville. Indeed, with its 9.5 acres of floor space, it was the largest single building in Eastern Washington. The adjacent vineyard was also quite impressive, with vines planted in a radical eye-popping pattern of circles instead of linear rows, designed to be irrigated by the type of wheeled center-pivot overhead sprinklers used on many wheat farms.

Doug Gore, 1982

Flying overhead on his way to the grand opening event, wine historian Leon D. Adams declared the spectacle a "viticultural miracle."[39] The newly hired Doug Gore had arrived just in time to help with the fall 1982 harvest and crush. For Gore it was the beginning of many years of making top-notch red wines at the old Grandview winery and overseeing the transport and storage of those barrels at River Ridge.

In the realm of white wines, River Ridge would focus on growing Chenin Blanc, Riesling, and additional white varieties that can be made without the use of oak barrels. Kay Simon was brought to River Ridge to take on the blending of the winery's Gewürztraminer, Muscat Canelli, and Riesling into a proprietary blend titled Columbia Crest (named after one of the summits of Mount Rainier). Simon's husband, Clay Mackey, was vineyard operations manager at River Ridge and Cold Creek.

Doug Gore had experience with Chateau Ste. Michelle back in the 1970s, when he was working for Beringer Vineyards in California. "Whenever they did Riesling tastings," he recalled, "we had Chateau Ste. Michelle Rieslings…[w]hich was highly unusual. But it was always among the best—if not *the* best—Riesling at the table." Gore took notice, and when he was called later from Woodinville about an assistant red winemaker job, "I came up…did interviews and got up to Washington in time for the 1982 harvest. It really was fortuitous."

Gore moved up to Prosser and quickly discovered that both the grape growing and winemaking processes were a bit behind the times. In the vineyards "drip irrigation was not fully developed yet. "There was still a lot of rill, or furrow, irrigation, which causes huge grapevines and huge canopies. We have learned since then," Gore explained. "We and the viticulturists at WSU did a lot of groundbreaking research back in the late '80s–early '90s, and we showed how you could conserve water, grow more varietally correct grapes, moderate the canopy, and still get a good crop load. We really had to struggle with these grapevines because of how they'd been managed and irrigated. They didn't express the best you could get from the vineyards."

Soon after Gore's arrival, the winery upgraded to new grape presses, "which give you better quality juice and therefore far better quality wine. That was a big step up in technology, [which] has played such a great role [in our process]. We are early adopters of technology—where appropriate," he said.

Gore was a key figure in the huge success of the Columbia Crest wines and his role in the company naturally expanded over the years. As executive VP of winemaking, vineyards and operations, Gore remains excited about the future: "It's been a great opportunity. I've…seen this whole crazy grape-growing wine industry of ours go from zero to the proverbial 100. It's very exciting for Chateau Ste. Michelle. But as good as we are, you haven't seen anything yet!"

COLUMBIA CREST WINERY

River Ridge faced some adversity in its first years. In fact, the vineyard partially froze in 1983. "We didn't even have enough grapes for the Ste. Michelle winery," Allen Shoup recalls, "so that huge facility just stayed vacant." The founding of River Ridge was a bold move, despite not being able to use its capacity immediately. Initially the timing was too good to resist, because in 1984 the Columbia Valley was officially designated as an AVA appellation and the market would increasingly place value on wines with labels citing these vineyard sources. Indeed, over time this would become Chateau Ste. Michelle's secret weapon. As Bob Betz noted, "To me, ultimately the hero of the story is the Columbia Valley. It was because of the physical reality—the growing conditions there—that we could make good wine back then." The company's early investment in the Columbia Valley ultimately cemented Chateau Ste. Michelle's commitment to the larger potential of the Washington wine business.

The idyllic setting at Columbia Crest Winery

But a few tough lessons were learned before the winery's long-term goals came to fruition. Columbia Crest sales did not meet expectations early on. Ted Baseler was among those who began thinking that the whole concept should be reconsidered. "One of the projects when I first got here was creating the Columbia Crest Winery and brand." The original graphic was a relief map of Washington State with the name "Columbia Crest by Ste. Michelle." Baseler thought that was a bit cumbersome, so he did some consumer research to learn more about how people reacted to the graphic. "People from Washington said: 'Oh, that's *great!* That's our state map.' But everybody from out of state said, 'I would never buy that; that's a terrible idea.'"

The graphics needed to reach out to that larger audience, but Baseler also concluded that it might be better to simplify the name to Columbia Crest Winery. "It made no sense to have two or three Chateau Ste. Michelle wineries when you've already got a distinct and very successful brand," he said. Renamed and rebranded, Columbia Crest eventually came out with a full line of varietals. "We rode the Merlot wave and it was wildly successful," said Baseler. "It was Chateau Ste. Michelle's first million-case-per-year winery, and that allowed us to reposition the Chateau Ste. Michelle brand to a higher level…[N]ow we had this competing varietal winery, Columbia Crest—with high quality at fair prices—and it transformed our company dramatically."

Columbia Crest's vineyards overlook the Columbia River.

With very good wines that were getting better all the time, Columbia Crest was successfully positioned as the less-traditional younger sibling to Chateau Ste. Michelle. "What's interesting," Baseler notes, "is that there is this dynamic in the business, of the traditional and the contemporary. Chateau Ste. Michelle is obviously [in] that traditional category, whereas Columbia Crest occupied a different space. It allowed us to have this very modern brand that was new on the scene, and it just exploded." In 1985 alone the winery shipped 175,000 cases.

It didn't hurt that Baseler was able to arrange for a string of celebrity endorsers for Columbia Crest that included the famed chef Bobby Flay and the Northwest's top TV chef, Jeff Smith (aka the "Frugal Gourmet"). In the right place at the right time to ride a new consumer trend, Columbia Crest soon established itself as the largest producer of Merlot in the nation. Ray Einberger took over the helm as head winemaker from 2003-2011. Today, winemaker Juan Muñoz-Oca is leading Columbia Crest in the winery's next chapter of Washington wine leadership and innovation.

CHATEAU STE. MICHELLE
SUMMER CONCERT SERIES

Chateau Ste. Michelle has long understood the value of creating new reasons for visitors to return again and again to the Woodinville winery.

As early as July 1979 the Northwest Chamber Orchestra was invited to the Chateau to perform Vivaldi's *Four Seasons* during a wine-dinner event in the Barrel Room. That same month, the Everett Symphony Orchestra and the Bellevue Philharmonic Orchestra also performed there. By September, Chateau Ste. Michelle had made the winery and grounds available for a benefit concert by six different chamber ensembles to raise funds in support of the struggling Seattle Philharmonic Orchestra.

Preparing for the show as hot-air balloons drift overhead

Red & white
concert night

In 1983 the winery built a small deck on the lawn just southwest of the Chateau. Ted Baseler recalled that Karen Mack, the visitors services director, asked him if they could host a concert. She estimated they would have maybe 150 people. After the event she told him, "It was a resounding success, we had over 200 people!" By 1985 the company was marketing that outdoor space as the "amphitheater." The concert schedule slowly grew, and because it was becoming clear that concert attendees also enjoyed buying wine, the notion of staging a regularly occurring summer series emerged naturally.

In the summer of 1986 a reported 5,000 people arrived at the amphitheater for a big bluegrass concert—and by 1988 the concert series was branded the "Chateau Ste. Michelle Summer Festival," which would present a variety of shows annually from May to September. In 1992 an expanded stage was unveiled, along with improved grounds, parking lots, and access roads. In 1994 the series was recast as the "Summer Festival on the Green." By 1996 the series was booking top-tier artists and over the years has established itself as one of the Seattle area's major summer events.

Attending these hundreds of shows has become a fond tradition for countless music fans and a broad array of legendary musicians as well as up-and-coming acts. The long list of music icons includes: Ray Charles, Tony Bennett, B. B. King, Bob Dylan, Paul Simon, Ringo Starr, the Beach Boys, the Temptations, the Four Tops, Merle Haggard, Stevie Wonder, Gladys Knight, Steve Winwood, John Fogerty, Crosby, Stills & Nash, Linda Ronstadt, Steely Dan, Emmylou Harris, Bonnie Raitt, Elvis Costello, Blondie, Devo, Wynton Marsalis, Julio Iglesias, Harry Conick Jr., Don Henley, Robert Plant, Alison Krauss & Union Station, John Legend, and the Dave Matthews Band.

The Summer Concert series has become an important philanthropic tradition. Net proceeds from the annual lineup help fund Chateau Ste. Michelle's charitable contributions program, benefiting some 400 nonprofit organizations, something that Baseler takes great pride in. "We host the Summer Concert series for the community and use it as a way to help fund great nonprofit organizations locally and nationally."

STIMSON LANE VINEYARDS AND ESTATES

At about this same time, Ste. Michelle's parent company founded a new holding company in which to manage their wine-related properties. Stimson Lane Wine & Spirits, Ltd. was named in honor of Frederick Stimson's old Hollywood Farm estate in Woodinville, whose original street address was One Stimson Lane.

Over the years, Chateau Ste. Michelle would launch many new initiatives, programs, and products—including starting its own Summer Concert Series in the winery's 4,300-capacity on-site amphitheater—and produce so many award-winning wines that the accomplishments of this period can be dizzying to review.

WHIDBEY'S ISLAND PORT OF CALL

Chateau Ste. Michelle broadened its public outreach by opening a satellite tasting room at Joe Molz's historic Greenbank Farm on Whidbey Island in 1984. The company simultaneously launched a new Cabernet-based dessert beverage, "Whidbey's Port," produced by Columbia Crest's winemaker Doug Gore, who "had no experience making Port-style wine. It is produced by adding brandy partway through fermentation, with the resulting wine being sweet and high in alcohol. 'Making that Port the first time was nerve-wracking,' Gore said. 'It's a little touchy. You want to have the right amount of alcohol and sweetness in the wine.'" A bit daunted by the task, Gore resorted to seeking advice from a former mentor back in California. "He encouraged me to do it. He warned me that the first time you do it, you won't sleep—and he was right. It's fun, it's interesting, and I enjoyed the heck out of making it."[40]

Greenbank Farm,
Whidbey Island

Molz' loganberry farm at Greenbank—long touted as the largest in the world—also provided the key ingredient for Chateau Ste. Michelle's Whidbey's Loganberry Liqueur. In a sense, this brought the Washington wine story full circle, with a nod to the sweet and fruity non-*vinifera* types originally favored by NAWICO and Pommerelle.

LEARNING FROM CHALLENGES

One of Chateau Ste. Michelle's core pursuits continued to be how best to grow *vinifera* grapes in Washington. In 1986 the winery hired a freshly graduated horticulturist from Washington State University, Kevin Corliss. The son of a Prosser-based Concord grape vineyard owner, Corliss seemed to have grape juice running in his veins. But as

Kevin Corliss at Cold Creek Vineyard

a scientist he was comfortable with facing the facts about the state of the still-young industry. "Most of us were just making this up as we went. Back then there was a huge unknown about how [to] take care of grapes in Eastern Washington," he said. "For example, we had the early plantings at River Ridge planted in circles under center-pivot irrigation systems. That's a *horrible* way to grow grapes! You use a lot of water and there are high pumping costs. So finally, we converted them to drip. But back in the day we didn't know. And the model they were using to plant was kind of "over hill over dale," down through the draws and everything. We learned a lesson from that: You don't plant in draws in Washington because it's cold down there. Over the course of the years, we've been pulling those vines out and leaving them wide open so the cold air can move out of the vineyards."

As a boy, Corliss crossed paths with Dr. Walter Clore. "He actually had a test-plot of grapes in my father's vineyard. I remember him coming out to work on that." During his horticulture studies at WSU, Corliss did an internship at Chateau Ste. Michelle's Grandview winery. Three years later, college degree in hand, he was hired as the winery's research viticulturist. Corliss and Clore's relationship continued: "He was like a walking encyclopedia of grapes. He could answer almost any question.

And if he couldn't answer it, the next day I would receive a folder with a bunch of information. He was a wonderful guy to go out in the vineyard with. But on top of that, he was such a great guy." As the years went by, Corliss' role expanded to managing all of Chateau Ste. Michelle's vineyards, as well as overseeing about 85 contracted vineyards in Washington and an additional 20 in Oregon.

As Chateau Ste. Michelle's VP of vineyards, Corliss has become one of the premier authorities on grape growing in Washington—one whose cooperative research with WSU has led to advances in irrigation practices, vineyard sustainability, and integrated pest management.

QUALITY-INSPIRED INNOVATIONS

Not only were the number of vineyards and wineries increasing dramatically, but the quality of wine was reaching levels no one thought possible. With more and more wineries winning international awards and achieving the highest scores and ratings, the entire region rose to a new level of winemaking.

"Great wineries like Leonetti, Woodward Canyon, and Quilceda Creek began creating phenomenal wines in the late 1980s," enthused Ted Baseler. It became clear that it was possible to make world-class wines in Washington. These successes motivated Ste. Michelle to push their wines even further—implementing an intensive Total Quality Management program and investing millions of dollars into French oak barrels.

It was 1990 and winemaker Mike Januik had just come on board. Chateau Ste. Michelle began a process of understanding the empirical process of winemaking to a whole new degree: emphasizing analysis and benchmarking against the great wines of Bordeaux and Burgundy. "I would say that may have been the single biggest initiative we ever did," said Baseler. Using Total Quality Management principles, the company continued tasting, examining, and gaining further understanding about the amount of oak, the types of oak used, the grapes, and the yield for optimum quality. Januik and the Chateau Ste. Michelle team considered qualities such as aroma, mid-palate, and finish to break down and systematically understand the nature of great wine.

The Chateau at night

Chapter Seven

BRANCHING OUT
WASHINGTON WINE MATURES

Much of the increasing buzz about Washington wines had to do with the fact that there were now finally enough wineries in existence—62 by 1987—to make wine country vacation touring a feasible option for travelers to Eastern Washington. In addition to a handful of survivors from the 1970s, there came a new wave of wineries, including: Abeja, Buty, Cayuse, Dunham Cellars, Fidélitas, Hedges Family Estate, K Vintners, Reininger, Rulo, Spring Valley Vineyard, Syncline Wine Cellars, and Walla Walla Vintners, among others who would routinely astound experts, winning regional, national, and international awards.

At the same time, more wineries were popping up on the west side of the Cascade Mountain Range, including: Andrew Will (Vashon Island), Cadence Winery (Seattle), Fidalgo Island Winery (Anacortes), McCrea Cellars (Seattle), Newton & Newton (Seattle), and Pacific Crest Wine Cellars (Marysville)—enough to keep things interesting for the wine-loving public. Especially in the Woodinville area.

WOODINVILLE WINE COUNTRY

The Chateau Ste. Michelle winery continued to win a place in the hearts and minds of the ever-increasing numbers of people now enjoying Washington wines and the grandeur of the estate and its grounds. The Stimson estate and gardens had been successfully listed on the National Register of Historical Places in 1980. By the mid-1980s it was receiving 250,000 visitors annually, many of them from out of state.

Chateau Ste. Michelle

Indeed, the winery's presence just outside of Woodinville was now having a huge impact. Formerly a farming community, the town was quickly transformed by the traffic of wine-touring visitors. Not surprisingly, other wineries began to migrate to the area, including Haviland Vintners, which built its headquarters directly across the road from the entrance to the Chateau in 1981. That facility was sold in 1987 to Columbia Winery, the successor of the Associated Vintners operation. The trickle became a flood of new arrivals as Woodinville became the Puget Sound region's wine-business destination. Today over 130 wineries and tasting rooms base themselves in this ever-growing community, including: Basel Cellars, Betz Family Winery, Brian Carter Cellars, DeLille Cellars, Fidélitas Wines, Goose Ridge Estate Winery, Gorman Winery, Januik Winery/Novelty Hill, Long Shadows, Mark Ryan Winery, and Matthews Estate. A host of breweries and distilleries are clustered nearby as well, feeding off the more than 300,000 visitors who visit the Chateau each year.

Bob Betz founded Betz Family Winery in 1997. He ran the business while still working for Chateau Ste. Michelle, before retiring six years later to focus solely on the family winery. Simultaneously, Betz earned his degree in 1998 as a Master of Wine (MW), a designation awarded by the Institute of Wine in London—a professional status only 278 other people in the world held at the time. Betz remains extremely thankful for the support he received from Chateau Ste. Michelle, his employer of 28 years.

Chateau Ste. Michelle
winery grounds

"As a small winery, I think we all owe an enormous debt of gratitude to the company: to marketing; to sales; to vineyards; to cellar. I never realized it as much until I retired from Chateau Ste. Michelle and dedicated myself to Betz Family Winery. Ste. Michelle is a great company, with absolutely top-notch people. And we are lucky as an industry to have them here."

NEW HIRES, NEW VINEYARDS, NEW ALLIANCES

As time went on some members of the Chateau Ste. Michelle team branched out to play other key roles in the region's wine history—some, of course, to found their own notable wineries. Meanwhile, new talent was brought aboard and new partnerships were forged with top-tier wine luminaries across the globe. One of the brightest talents at Chateau Ste. Michelle during the 1990s was food and wine expert John Sarich, who had started working at the company as an entry-level tour guide during the opening season of 1976 and became the winery's resident culinary director in 1990.

JOHN SARICH

John Sarich

Soon after starting his Ste. Michelle career as a winery tour guide, John Sarich's natural star power became obvious to the entire team. Sarich soon moved to sales and was a food and wine consultant to restaurant chefs. In the 1980s he even opened his own restaurants in Seattle. His Adriatica, located above Lake Union, was a hit and *Esquire* magazine saluted Sarich as one of America's "hot new chefs."

But Sarich loved Ste. Michelle. In 1990 he returned to serve as the winery's culinary director. The *Seattle Times* credited him as "Washington's first and most prolific wine-and-food ambassador," one who "set a precedent by becoming the first full-time chef at a Northwest winery."[41] Sarich would go on to pen cookbooks, including *Chef in the Vineyard* and *John Sarich at Chateau Ste. Michelle: For Cooks Who Love Wine*. He also hosted his own Emmy-nominated KIRO-TV cooking show, *Taste of the Northwest*, shot live in the winery's kitchen during its four-year run.

Upon his sudden passing in October 2014, a Ste. Michelle executive would eulogize Sarich saying: "John was a beloved and legendary member of the Chateau Ste. Michelle family and Washington wine and culinary community. John spent the last three decades inspiring and educating people around the world with his passion for food and wine through his TV shows, cookbooks, and Chateau Ste. Michelle culinary events. He had a tremendous talent and infectious enthusiasm for helping people learn about and enjoy the pleasures of wine and food."[42] Chateau Ste. Michelle established the John R. Sarich Jr. Memorial Scholarship at the Seattle Culinary Academy in honor of Sarich and his remarkable life and career.

During that same year of 1990, Mike Januik and Charlie Hoppes joined Chateau Ste. Michelle after working together at Snoqualmie Winery. Hoppes was named assistant winemaker, and later red winemaker. A Wapato, Washington, native who'd picked Concords as a high schooler, Hoppes went on study at UC Davis before working with Mike Januik at Snoqualmie.

Januik was also UC Davis-trained, with a master's degree in fermentation science. Januik's talent was a good match for Chateau Ste. Michelle's resources and goals. "I had so many great opportunities at Ste. Michelle while I was there. They were very focused on the idea of doing whatever they could to improve the quality of wine that was being produced. And…they pretty much gave me carte blanche to do whatever I thought was necessary to achieve that goal," he said. "For example, the whole French oak barrel program was increased significantly. Not just in terms of the number of new barrels we used. For instance, we started barrel fermentation of 100 percent of the Chardonnay that we were producing. That was 15,000 barrels! That hadn't been done previously and was a big leap up." So too would be a new focus on making wines from grapes grown in specific, and notable, single vineyards.

Mike Januik, 1981

"The first single vineyard growing I made was in 1991," said Januik. "It was Merlot from Indian Wells Vineyard, and we just kept expanding that program, and that was *real* positive." Januik would ultimately be responsible for a decade of fine winemaking at Chateau Ste. Michelle. In January 1991 Ste. Michelle bought the Snoqualmie/Langguth Winery but kept the [Snoqualmie] brand going with wines made by Joy Andersen at the Columbia Crest winery.

Chateau Ste. Michelle began planting their 559-acre Canoe Ridge Estate Vineyard in the Horse Heaven Hills AVA in 1991, and Ron Bunnell was brought in to assist with red wines, while Erik Olsen was hired to help make whites. Like Hoppes and Januik, Bunnell and Olsen were from UC Davis and brought substantial California winery experience and academic training to their tasks. In 1993, while Canoe Ridge Estate's new winery was being built, accolades for Bunnell and Olsen's early wines started pouring in, with Robert Parker rating the 1991 Indian Wells Merlot as being "World Class," and Richard Nalley, the nationally syndicated wine columnist, pegging it as the number one wine in America.

Chateau Ste. Michelle launched another successful endeavor in 1993: their annual *Artist Series* of Bordeaux-style red wines with labels featuring well-known artists. The Pacific Northwest's superstar glassblowing artist Dale Chihuly—whose work is also on display at the Chateau—was the inaugural artist. Mike Januik, who was the winemaker for the first several releases recalled, "It was really interesting, because I got to interact with the artists and spend time with them."

The year 1995 saw the debut release of a new "internationally styled" red wine, Col Solare, made by Januik at the Canoe Ridge Estate winery, using Washington grapes in a promising new partnership project with the Tuscan winemaking legend, Marchese Piero Antinori. Col Solare is a luxurious Cabernet Sauvignon-based blend that is created from estate-grown fruit at the Tuscan-style winery built in 2007 on Washington's esteemed Red Mountain. It was the first of several important international partnerships that have defined Chateau Ste. Michelle's recent history.

CANOE RIDGE ESTATE WINERY
AND VINEYARD

The very name of Canoe Ridge Estate evokes the deep history of the area where this treasured vineyard is situated. The ridge itself looms above the Columbia River shoreline along its southern edge, and ranges eastward from upstream of Alder Creek and westward to the Blalock Islands. In October of 1805, Captain Meriwether Lewis and Second Lieutenant William Clark's Corp of Discovery expedition paddled their canoes downstream through the Blalock Islands, noting the area's features as they went along. Legend holds that one of their team commented that the ridge to the north resembled an overturned canoe.

Canoe Ridge Estate

Vineyard

The south-facing slope of Canoe Ridge Estate Vineyard consists of well-drained deep, sandy loam soil and cobblestone. Vineyard elevations now rise up to 950 feet above sea level. The vineyard is warm, but its temperatures are moderated by the Columbia River. As Mimi Nye, the longtime Canoe Ridge Estate Vineyard manager, enthused, "This is a great place to grow grapes for a few reasons. For one thing: we're right along the Columbia and it provides warmth for the vines in the wintertime. They don't like to be cold, and the river provides just a little bit of heat [to the vineyards]."

Average annual rainfall here of six inches, combined with low-fertility soils, constant sun, and steady winds coming up from the Columbia River provide the perfect model for premium grape growing. The soil is built upon ancient basalt and as described by Nye, "It's basically the remains of a lava flow that was deposited about 9 million years ago. But there are other rocks we find here—from Montana and Canada—which flowed in on glacial ice during the last Ice Age. And the sand and gravel soil here was brought in by the great Missoula floods. But flood soils are poor. And that's actually good for grapes, because you want grapes to struggle and not have too much of a cushy life. Like with people, stress actually builds character into the wine."

Canoe Ridge Estate Vineyard was planted in 1991 and today its 559 acres consist of Cabernet Sauvignon, Chardonnay, Merlot, and Syrah grapes.

With Chateau Ste. Michelle's growth in the late 1980s, the winery outgrew their Woodinville cellar. The company decided to build a dedicated red wine facility which opened for harvest in 1994 at the site of its Canoe Ridge Estate Vineyard. Led by red winemaker Raymon McKee, the Canoe Ridge Estate winery is specifically customized for red wine production and includes a Reserve Cellar, featuring state-of-the art sorting and fermentation equipment for maximum quality. Both the Canoe Ridge Estate winery and vineyard have earned LIVE sustainability certification—an internationally recognized certification of sustainable wine growing and winemaking practices. The Canoe Ridge Estate winery gained that status beginning with the 2013 vintage.

As one of the preeminent vineyard sites in the Horse Heaven Hills AVA, Canoe Ridge produces grapes that result in elegant, refined wines featuring intense concentration and structure. Earning scores of 90 points or higher on more than 40 of their wines, Chateau Ste. Michelle's Canoe Ridge Estate Vineyard Chardonnay, Cabernet Sauvignon, and Merlot have each received *Wine Spectator* magazine's "Top 100" honors.

Canoe Ridge Estate

THE ARTIST SERIES

Chateau Ste. Michelle spotlighted the art of winemaking in 1993 by pairing the work of a gifted winemaker with that of a master fine artist in the launch of their *Artist Series* bottlings. Each year a renowned artist is honored with beautiful labels featuring his or her artwork, from blown glass to bronze sculptures to paint on canvas.

Head Winemaker Bob Bertheau, who began crafting the Artist Series wines several years in, explained, "At the end of the season we evaluate all the wines. We taste every single lot. And occasionally, one of the blocks of grapes says 'Artist Series' to me. This doesn't mean that it's the biggest wine, it means it's an *interesting* wine with layers and complexity and a little bit of what I call that 'powdery Bordeaux' style of tannin. It's not about showing the power of Washington—though we have some wines that do that. [T]he vision of this wine is to be more like an artist and show complexity and nuance and layering of flavors within the context of Washington State fruit."

It is an inspiring project for all concerned. As Bertheau described, "I feel like an artist when we're blending—and our medium just happens to be all this wonderful Washington fruit." Fine wine lovers and art aficionados agree, and the *Artist Series* has emerged as an incredible annual success, with the wines dependably earning 90+ ratings by numerous top critics. The artists who have participated in this exciting program since its inception include a unique treasure of talent.

Dale Chihuly
Artist Series

1993: Dale Chihuly

1994: William Morris

1995: Lino Tagliapietra

1996: Ginny Ruffner

1997: Dan Dailey

1998: Flora C. Mace
     and Joey Kirkpatrick

1999: Stanislav
     Libenský and
     Jaroslava Brychtová

2000: Italo Scanga

2001: Richard Marquis

2002: Gerard
     Tsutakawa

2003: Will Robinson

2004: Alden Mason

2005: Bobbie Burgers

2006: Eva Isaksen

2007: T. L. Lange

2008: Cara Barer

2009: Andre Petterson

2010: Ben Darby

2011: Bratsa Bonifacho

2012: Dale Chihuly

2013: Cameron Anne
     Mason

2014: Janna Watson

WINEMAKING PARTNERSHIPS

Among the most exciting endeavors Chateau Ste. Michelle has launched in recent years are the partnerships forged with an array of celebrated vintners hailing from some of the world's finest wine regions. As the first winery to introduce international partners to Washington, Chateau Ste. Michelle blazed a trail that has led to collaborative creativity with winemaking luminaries from historic wine countries such as Italy, Germany, and France. This nexus of Old World enological and viticultural experience, coupled with the expertise of Chateau Ste. Michelle's teams and the unique aspects of Washington vineyards and grapes, has resulted in innovative practices and stunning wines.

COL SOLARE AND THE ANTINORI FAMILY

Marchese Piero Antinori is the patriarch of a remarkable Italian family wine business that traces back 26 generations. The Antinori family was making wine before Columbus discovered America, with historical records in Florence listing the beginning of their business in the year 1385. As Ted Baseler recalled, "André Tchelistcheff introduced us to Piero Antinori, who he was consulting with in Italy. And he told Antinori: 'You have got to see what's happening in Washington State. It's remarkable the wines that are being created there!'" After Antinori's visit to Washington wine country in 1992, he had to agree: "The Columbia Valley has much in common with the best vineyards in the world, a unique combination of the right climates, sunlight, soil, and topography."[43]

Col Solare on
Red Mountain

Col Solare barrel room

"What impressed me about the wines of Washington was really the fact that the[y] were rather similar to the Old World wines in terms of style and elegance," said Antinori. "I felt at home there."[44] The alliance between Chateau Ste. Michelle and Antinori would prove to be a potent one. The partnership created Col Solare, Italian for "shining hill," in 1995. Its first releases were deemed "blockbusters" by the *Seattle Times*. Col Solare would go on to plant a 29-acre estate vineyard on Red Mountain in 2006, open its state-of-the-art winery there in 2007, and release its first Red Mountain-designated wine with the 2011 vintage.

The Antinori partnership also made it possible to acquire one of California wine country's crown jewels: Stag's Leap Wine Cellars. "Col Solare is one of many ventures for us," said Antinori, "and it is important because just as the Ste. Michelle viticulturists and winemakers learn from us, we learn from them. It is an excellent partnership."[45]

EROICA AND ERNST LOOSEN

Born into a family tradition of winemaking, Ernst Loosen was raised on a 50-acre vineyard estate situated along the Mosel River in Germany. In 1988 Loosen—who had studied enology at the famed school in Geisenheim—assumed control of the Dr. Loosen Estate, which had been in his family for over two centuries. The vineyards boasted Riesling vines that were then "well over 100 years old—vines perfectly suited to the low-yield, highly concentrated style he wanted to produce." Loosen furthered his education by traveling to many of the world's prime winemaking regions to immerse himself in the best practices being employed by the finest enologists and viticulturists. He discovered "that they all share a dedication to producing intense,

Ernst Loosen (left) and Bob Bertheau

concentrated wines that boldly proclaim their heritage." They also shared a passion for both traditional and modern winemaking techniques. Partnering with Chateau Ste. Michelle in 1999—after Loosen had been deeply impressed by the 1997 Cold Creek Vineyard Chardonnay—seemed a perfect match. With grapes from the Columbia Valley, the partnership has resulted in award-winning Eroica Riesling, Eroica Single

Eroica wines

Berry Select, and Eroica Gold wines. According to Loosen, "The Eroica Riesling collaboration with Chateau Ste. Michelle has been a remarkable journey. When we started it in 1999, our dream was that we'd be helping to return Riesling to its former high standing among the great wines of the world. But to see it actually happening—to see Riesling regaining its reputation as the most noble white wine variety and to know that we played some part in that—has been extremely rewarding."

The Eroica partnership has evolved into a true collaboration. Ernst Loosen and Bob Bertheau work together on decisions of site selection, irrigation management, crop levels, and canopy management. They work with vineyard managers and growers to adjust yields and manage fruit exposure to prolong the ripening of these cooler climate vineyards for added flavor development. At the blending table, Loosen and Bertheau consider dozens of small lots, each reflecting a slight difference in character, depending on where and how the fruit was grown. It is this blend of the finest Riesling fruit of the vintage that gives Eroica its remarkable complexity and character.

"It has been very interesting to see the evolution in winemaking style that has taken place with Eroica Riesling over nearly 20 years," said Loosen. "As we search for the best expression of Washington fruit and terroir, as well as respond to vintage variations and changing tastes internationally, the wine has become drier and more focused on minerality. I think we have found a nearly ideal balance…but I am excited to see how it continues to evolve in intensity and expressivity over the next 20 years."[46]

TENET: MICHEL GASSIER AND PHILIPPE CAMBIE

Back in the late 1980s, Ste. Michelle decided that it needed to understand the great wines of the world. The winery started importing excellent Bordeaux and Burgundies with the help of a young man named Michel Gassier. Though the importing business was not lucrative, it was an enlightening endeavor. Fast forward decades later to the 2010 Hong Kong Vin-Expo and a not-quite-as-young Michel Gassier approached Ted Baseler and reintroduced himself. Gassier had seen what Chateau Ste. Michelle had done with Antinori and Loosen and wanted to get involved in something similar. Baseler invited him to Washington State.

By that time, Chateau Ste. Michelle's team had developed a strong belief—or "tenet"—that Washington's Columbia Valley would prove to be a world-class area for growing the *vinifera* grapes long prized in the Rhône Valley of France. With the fundamentals of sand-over-basalt terroir and shared latitude already covered, the idea of a fruitful international partnership emerged. Chateau Ste. Michelle's Head Winemaker Bob Bertheau began a collaboration with Michel Gassier and enology consultant Phillipe Cambie. The Frenchmen brought expertise with "local techniques honed through centuries of experience with Rhône grapes in their birthplace, while the Chateau Ste. Michelle team provides expert knowledge of Washington fruit and the best in modern winemaking techniques." Working together, the three selected new cooler vineyard sites and applied Cambie's advice regarding canopy size and load and hand-harvesting grape clusters, as well as Gassier's recommendations regarding fermentation and maceration. "Inclusion of stems in fermentations…provides very specific and unique characteristics that are certainly a departure from more fruit–driven Chateau Ste. Michelle wines, as is the use of extended maceration.

Tenet Wines

These techniques lead to increased complexity and a different expression of terroir."

Among the remarkable wines produced by this partnership are the Tenet GSM, a Grenache/Syrah/Mourvèdre blend, and The Pundit Syrah. In addition, Gassier has crafted a companion wine, the "Le Fervent" Syrah, from the Costières de Nîmes AOC of the Rhône Valley. "In France, we have a long tradition of understanding and revealing the nature of terroir," said Gassier. "We partnered with Chateau Ste. Michelle and offered our experience to help get beautiful Rhône varietals with a very clear Washington signature." The project was an immediate success with the inaugural 2013 The Pundit Syrah making *Wine Spectator's* Top 100 list.[47]

Foliage on the Chateau

Ste. Michelle grounds

HIGH HONORS, WELL EARNED

Vintage after vintage Chateau Ste. Michelle has achieved increasing levels of acclaim, consistently garnering numerous laudatory critiques, medals, and awards.

1988: "Best American Winery," Tasters Guild and *Wine Country* magazine

1990: "Wine Producer of the Year," Robert Parker

1991: 1987 Cabernet Sauvignon awarded only gold medal for an American red wine at *VinExpo* in Bordeaux, France (June 1991)

Eighteen *Wine Spectator* "Top 100" wines, including the 1991 Late Harvest White Riesling Reserve (December 1995), 1993 Cold Creek Vineyard Chardonnay (December 1995), 1996 Cold Creek Vineyard Cabernet Sauvignon (December 2000), 1999 Canoe Ridge Estate Merlot (December 2002), 2003 Eroica Riesling (December 2004), 2006 Canoe Ridge Estate Cabernet Sauvignon (December 2009), and 2013 Tenet The Pundit Syrah (December 2015).

2001: 1999 Cold Creek Chardonnay ranked #16 in *Wine Spectator*'s "Top 100 Wines," the highest-ranked white wine in the world at the time (December 2001)

2003: 2000 Eroica Single Berry Select earns 98-point rating from *Wine Spectator*—the highest rating for any Washington wine at the time (April 2003)

2004: American Winery of the Year, *Wine Enthusiast* magazine (December 2004)

2005: Winery of the Year, *Restaurant Wine* (January 2005)

2008: Wine Brand of the Year, *Market Watch* magazine Leader's Choice Awards (October 2008)

2009: Columbia Crest 2005 Reserve Cabernet Sauvignon scored 95 points and crowned "#1 Wine of the Year" by *Wine Spectator*—the first Washington wine to receive this honor (November 2009)

Columbia Valley wines

2011: Washington's Most Respected Brand, *Puget Sound Business Journal* (August 2011)

2011: Winery of the Year, Wine.com (January 2012)

2013: Pacific Northwest Winery of the Year, *Wine Press Northwest* (March 2013)

2016: U.S. Producer of the Year, International Wine & Spirits Competition (November 2016)

Twenty-two "Wineries of the Year" honors by *Wine & Spirits*, making it the publication's most-awarded American winery (Winter 2016)

A NEW MILLENNIUM DAWNS

In 1999 construction began at Chateau Ste. Michelle on a new barrel room for white wines, while an expansion of the Canoe Ridge Estate red wine winery also commenced. That same year winemaker Mike Januik moved on to start up his own namesake winery, while Ron Bunnell replaced Charlie Hoppes as head red winemaker at Canoe Ridge Estate.

As Chateau Ste. Michelle entered its fourth decade, the stunning pace of progress continued. In early 2001 Allen Shoup stepped aside and Ted Baseler—who had advanced from VP of marketing to executive VP of sales, marketing, and communications—was promoted to the position of president and CEO. "I had been here for almost sixteen years and one of the advantages I had was knowing all of the inner workings from an operational perspective. The first initiative was to reduce costs and to do it *thoughtfully*. For example, we used to painstakingly pack all of our Reserve wines in wood cases. But when we went out and talked to our customers, particularly the restaurants, they informed us that [the cases were] a pain in the neck because they would have to get a crowbar to pry [them] open. Here we were spending millions of dollars on these wood boxes, and our customers didn't even *want* them. Those are the kinds of things we were able to fine-tune to improve service and add value to our customers."

Piero Antinori and Ste. Michelle CEO Baseler toasting at the grand opening of Col Solare, April 12, 2007

Another important step Baseler took when he became CEO was to bridge the gap between the grape growing and vineyard sides of the business in Eastern Washington and the Chateau's production and consumer sides in Western Washington. During Baseler's many meetings and focus groups, he found that many people in the company felt they were low on the totem pole; that someone on the other side of the mountains called the shots. Baseler worked hard to change the approach and attitude. He convinced folks that whatever they did, their job—and their role—was important. Part of the answer was implementing quarterly meetings with the whole company. "People really want to know how our company

Grape harvesting, 2014

is doing and want a regular meeting to understand the status. They put their blood, sweat, and tears into the business and they want to know if it is working. One of the things we do is welcome all of our new employees. After they are introduced, I stand up and yell, 'Welcome to the best damned wine company in the world!' and a cheer goes up. It has become kind of a tradition." The company hasn't missed a quarterly meeting in the 17 years since they began.

In 2003 Erik Olsen moved on to the Vice President/Winemaker position at California's Clos du Bois Winery and Bob Bertheau was brought aboard as white winemaker. Bertheau's elegant Ethos Reserve Chardonnay consistently slayed the critics, and in 2004 *Wine Enthusiast* magazine saluted Chateau Ste. Michelle as its "American Winery of the Year."

Chateau Ste. Michelle white winemaker David Rosenthal tests wine.

BOB BERTHEAU

Chateau Ste. Michelle's head winemaker since 2004, Bob Bertheau has now served in that role longer than any previous winemaker. A Seattle native, Bertheau was aiming for a medical degree while studying chemistry at Boise State University when he scored a part-time weekend job pouring in the Ste. Chapelle Winery tasting room in town. Bertheau's exposure to the wine world inspired him to change directions after earning his chemistry degree. He went on to earn a master's degree in food science and enology at UC Davis. While in California, Bertheau worked at several wineries, including Hanzell Vineyards, Chalk Hill, and Gallo Sonoma, where he helped the large producer craft a more artisanal approach to winemaking.

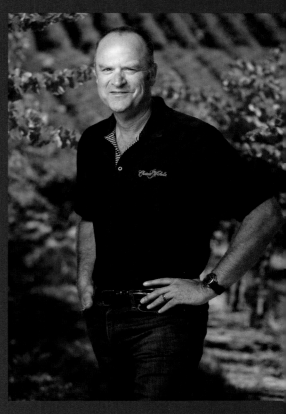

Bob Bertheau

Bertheau returned home to the Pacific Northwest to join Chateau Ste. Michelle in 2003 with 16 years of experience in the wine industry under his belt. He brought to the table a scientific background, an artist's heart, and a deep understanding of making quality wines—especially Chardonnay. When, during his job interview, he'd been asked "Have you made any Riesling?" he answered breezily "Oh, yeah, of course." But on his second day, when Doug Gore assigned him to pick up Ernst Loosen at the Pasco, Washington, airport, Bertheau admitted feeling a bit of trepidation. Here he was, suddenly working for the largest producer of top-quality Riesling in the world, about to meet the world renowned German Riesling expert and, in perfect truth, he had made exactly *one* tank of Riesling in his whole career. "It was a little daunting. But good fruit and good protocols were already in place here and I had Erni Loosen as my mentor literally from day two on the job. I gained a lot of knowledge just by tasting with him and listening to him." During their first of many years of "vineyard walks," the two met growers of the key blocks of vines and examined the vines' developmental progress.

Bertheau's debut 2003 Riesling proved to be a winner, and his collaborations with Loosen on the Eroica wines raised the bar for Washington wine quality. In 2004 Bertheau advanced to Chateau Ste. Michelle's head winemaker position and swiftly began managing such elite lines as the Artist Series Meritage Red, Ethos Reserve Cabernet, Limited Release club wines, and many others. Bertheau remembers a key concept that Ste. Michelle's CEO shared with him. "Ted Baseler said to me when I was first hired: 'Yes, you are the [Chateau] Ste. Michelle winemaker. But…when you go out to talk to the market, you talk about Washington State first, and *then* you talk about the brand. Because that, honestly, is how we are set up for success: We highlight our vineyards and sense of place more than brands and people.'"

HARVESTING SUCCESS
STE. MICHELLE WINE ESTATES, INC.

To better reflect both its rich history and ambitious vision for the future, in 2004 Chateau Ste. Michelle's parent corporation changed the name of its holding company from Stimson Lane to Ste. Michelle Wine Estates (SMWE). The move was part of a future that would see the company continue to forge strategic alliances, improve its Chateau winery and grounds, acquire promising small wineries, and add select vineyard properties to its growing portfolio.

That same year, Bob Bertheau was promoted to head winemaker and Eroica earned its fifth *Wine Spectator* "Top 100 Wines" honor. Then in 2005 SMWE launched its new 14 Hands Winery—named for a breed of small now-extinct, native mustang ponies that were only about fourteen hand-widths high—with wines crafted by Keith Kenison that were aimed at the restaurant trade. *Restaurant Wine* magazine named Chateau Ste. Michelle the "American Winery of the Year" in 2005, and a year later the 2004 Canoe Ridge Estate Vineyard Chardonnay would go on to score again on the *Wine Spectator* "Top 100 Wines" list.

Chateau Ste. Michelle winery and Dr. Loosen estate cohosted an important three-day event in July 2007. Billed as "Riesling Rendezvous," it was an unprecedentedly large gathering of Riesling experts—73 producers from seven different countries—who successfully explored the versatility of Rieslings on a worldwide basis.

The Rendezvous was such a success, it would be repeated over subsequent years. Another momentous milestone occurred that same year: after 15 years of exclusive availability in the Pacific Northwest, the Chateau Ste. Michelle Dry Riesling was finally released nationwide.

One of Australia's best white winemakers, Wendy Stuckey, was recruited as the new White Winemaker in 2007. The following year, the 2007 Dry Riesling was named "Best Riesling of the New World" at the 2008 *International Riesling Competition* in Germany. Upon Stuckey's return to the Southern Hemisphere in 2015—to New Zealand—Assistant Winemaker David Rosenthal was promoted to white winemaker.

CEO Ted Baseler has developed an intriguing view of the business. As he leads Ste. Michelle Wine Estates' acquisition of wineries and vineyard properties to the portfolio, he views them as a treasured "string of pearls"—precious, unique wineries from throughout the world's finest wine regions, individually beautiful, yet strung together into a greater whole. Though associated, these wineries are encouraged to make their own decisions about their unique vines, grapes, and wines. The pearls include Chateau Ste. Michelle, Columbia Crest, 14 Hands, Northstar, Spring Valley Vineyard, and Col Solare in Washington and Erath in Oregon. In California the company also owns Stag's Leap Wine Cellars (with Italy's Antinori family), Conn Creek in the Napa Valley, and most recently the Sonoma-based gem Patz & Hall.

In addition to securing the exclusive American distributorship of Italian wines from Antinori—along with the wines produced by his partnership with the Matte family of Chile's esteemed Haras De Pirque winery—Ste. Michelle Wine Estates has

Guests mingle outside the chateau at the Riesling Rendezvous, 2016.

forged a similar arrangement for French Champagne from Nicolas Feuillatte and with New Zealand's most highly awarded winery, Villa Maria Estates. The company has also partnered with the venerable Bodegas Torres company, whose namesake family has made wine in Spain since 1870, owns that country's largest winery and also owns and operates the Miguel Torres winery in Chile.

Chateau Ste. Michelle was named "Wine Brand of the Year" in *Market Watch* magazine's "Leaders Choice Awards" in 2008; "Washington's Most Respected Brands" in the *Puget Sound Business Journal's* "Battle of the Brands" readers' poll in 2011; and "Winery of the Year" by the online wine retailer Wine.com. In 2012 it won the "United States Wine Producer of the Year" award at the International Wine and Spirit Competition, and in 2016 Chateau Ste. Michelle was named "Winery of the Year" by *Wine & Spirits* magazine for the 22nd time—more than any other American winery.

STE. MICHELLE GROWS UP AND SUPPORTS THE INDUSTRY

Ste. Michelle has blossomed into a truly remarkable enterprise over its first 50 years. It owns more than 3,800 vineyard acres in Washington, Oregon, and California, and holds long-term contracts for substantially more acreage. Its portfolio of prized holdings includes one of Oregon's founding firms, Erath Winery and the Willakia Vineyard. According to Baseler, "Our acquisition of the Willakia Vineyard demonstrates our commitment to upholding Erath's legacy as the leading Pinot Noir producer in Oregon…It is critical, of course, that we grow our own business by constantly improving on everything we do. Those improvements always lead back to wine quality and our ultimate purpose of creating wines with soul, character, and a sense of place."

In addition to producing undeniably fine wines, SMWE has served as an incubator for technological advances in viticulture and enology. It has also successfully discovered and nurtured young winemaking talents and assisted numerous younger wineries along the way. As the *Seattle Post-Intelligencer* once noted: "In the early years, when most local wineries had no marketing budgets, Ste. Michelle's sales representative would show other Washington wines as they traveled the country. During surplus years, growers were paid for fruit that would never be made into wine. In freeze years such as 1996, when crops were nearly wiped out, the Chateau sold some of its grapes to affected wineries."[48]

Chateau Ste. Michelle's Columbia Valley Cabernet Sauvignon

ALUMNI HONOR ROLL

Ste. Michelle takes great pride in the fact that it has nurtured countless talents who've risen up through its ranks. Among them: Allen Shoup, VP of marketing who rose to CEO and went on to found Long Shadows Vintners; Paul Shipman, brand manager who went on to co-found Seattle's Redhook Brewery, which helped kick-start the craft beer renaissance in 1981; Charles Finkel, VP of marketing who founded Seattle's Merchant du Vin and Pike Pub & Brewery; and Ted Baseler, VP of marketing who is now CEO. There have been more than a few winemakers who launched great careers at Ste. Michelle and subsequently branched off to launch their own wineries, such as Bob Betz (Betz Family Winery), Ron Bunnell (Bunnell Family Cellar), Stan Clarke (Quail Run Winery—today's Covey Run), Charlie Hoppes (Fidélitas Wines), Mike Januik (Januik Wines), Joel Klein (Snoqualmie Winery), Kay Simon (Chinook Wines), and Wade Wolfe (Thurston Wolfe Wines).

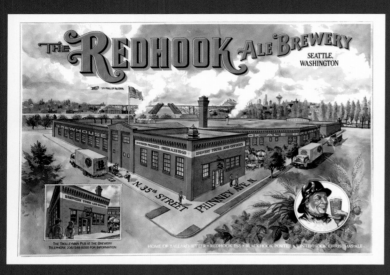

Redhook Brewery promotional poster, circa 1981

Another example of the winery's regional spirit was described by Mike Januik, who gave notice in 1999 that he would be leaving after nearly a decade to form his own namesake company. "Ste. Michelle gave me a lot of opportunities to excel in my career and go on to other things," he recently stated. "I don't think I would have been able to start my own winery if I hadn't had that experience there. I've always been very grateful." But even beyond providing such a great grounding in the big-time wine business, Ste. Michelle actually went further. "Ste. Michelle gave me a very generous consulting agreement for the next two years to work with the winemakers who were replacing me. As much as anything, they did it because they wanted to help me out, which it did."[49]

The company also allowed Januik to annually purchase grapes from their highly prized Cold Creek Vineyard. "Because of that, I decided to make Chardonnay and I've been making Chardonnay ever since from the Cold Creek Vineyard. And I've always appreciated that. I felt it was quite generous to do that." Indeed, any other winery would jealously covet access to those grapes. "To me it's an example of a larger company really demonstrating a level of thoughtfulness that you might not always expect."

The Stimson's
Manor House in
modern times

When an arctic blast hit Washington in 2004, Marty Clubb, the winemaker and co-owner at Walla Walla's L'Ecole No. 41 Winery, recalled how when the temperature suddenly plunged to 15 degrees it ruined that year's harvest, "We had basically no crop," he said. "We were facing catastrophe." And then his phone rang. It was Ted Baseler. As Baseler would later recall: "We called lots of wineries and said 'Hey listen: you guys need grapes, we'll get you grapes. And we will help you make wine this year. Because we *want* you to be in business. We want you to be successful.' That was really surprising to a lot of people. Not to me. I don't understand why we wouldn't have done that, but some people don't think that way." Trey Busch, then winemaker at Basel Cellars Estate Winery was impressed. "Ted was reaching a hand out to all the wineries. I can't imagine anybody in Napa Valley doing that."[50]

According to Baseler, "Our business philosophy has always been to help the industry *and* to be at the forefront. I think that we've demonstrated much more of a collegial approach to business. Principally because we want to grow the Washington State category. We're not focused on market share. We're not trying to beat out some little guy. It makes no sense. Collectively, we do much better together. I think most people would agree with that thesis. I mean, there are probably a few people who are struggling that might think we're the big 800-pound gorilla here, but the vast majority understand our investment in the business and what we are willing to do. Oftentimes we'll forego our own identity or success for the good of the industry."

The simple fact is that Ste. Michelle has proven to be a visionary company, with a far-ranging view of things. "It has spent millions of dollars on research and development and shared the results with other wineries. Countless industry and community projects have been quietly bankrolled by the company."[51]

For years the company has been a prime sponsor of the Auction of Washington Wines annual charity events and raising millions for Seattle's Children's Hospital. During its 29th year in 2016, the auction raised over $3 million. The company also supports Washington State University's Ste. Michelle Wine Estates Wine Science Center and funds the Chateau Ste. Michelle Diversity College Scholarship Fund for underserved students at Washington universities.

THE STE. MICHELLE WINE ESTATES WINE SCIENCE CENTER

As far back as the early 1980s, the Washington State Legislature enacted legislation that taxed in-state wineries (at a rate of 1/4 cent per liter of wine sold) to help fund research programs in viticulture, enology, and agricultural economics at Washington State University (WSU). It also stipulated that the Washington wine industry provide WSU with recommendations for research topics, which led to the founding of the Wine Research Advisory Committee and the 1987 founding of a new agency, the Washington Wine Commission. In addition, in 2003 the state of Washington also committed to providing $2.3 million (per biennium) in order to fund the creation of two- and four-year degree programs to support the technical needs of the wine industry—a move that the Washington Wine Institute supported and celebrated.

As the wine business boomed over the years, the need for an even greater focus on research became clear. In 2011 the industry, led by Ste. Michelle, voluntarily voted to increase their annual assessments to better fund a dedicated wine science center. As Baseler proudly notes, "We invested a lot of time and money in helping create this world-class center. The University of California, Davis was phenomenally helpful.

Ste. Michelle Wine Estates WSU Wine Science Center

Kind of *shockingly* helpful, because they have always had kind of a corner on the market for enology and viticulture education. When I asked them why they were so supportive of our programs they said, 'It's not a competition. There should be at least a dozen centers in the United States. Now there will be two!'"

The unsurpassed support that Baseler and Ste. Michelle offered the project has already been rewarded. WSU held a grand opening event for their new state-of-the-art research and educational institution in June 2015, proudly naming it the Ste. Michelle Wine Estates Wine Science Center. Set on the WSU Tri-Cities campus in Richland, in the heart of Washington wine country, it "is equal to those at other top research universities worldwide and ready to serve as a gathering place to spark innovation, fuel economic development, support local, regional, national and international collaboration, and provide a catalyst for research breakthroughs."

Interior of WSU Wine Science Center

The Center's goal is to help steer the Washington wine industry toward more environmentally sustainable practices and economic success. As Baseler confirms, "In considering the future of the industry, this is going to be a cornerstone of excellence. Its impact on the quality of Washington wines in the future will be tremendous. For me, it is very exciting to have that as part of our contribution to the wine industry."

Kevin Corliss, Ste. Michelle's VP of vineyard operations, is personally thrilled about the current state of the Washington wine business: "I just pinch myself sometimes when looking back. You know, I got to go through the birth of a real industry. And now the Wine Science Center enology program has helped energize the next generation coming along. When I was at WSU, there were about 50 students in the horticulture program: about 25 of them were going to do flowers or vegetables in Western Washington, and about 24 of them were going to do tree-fruits in Wenatchee. Only one of them was interested in grapes—and that was me! I was the only crazy guy who wanted to do *grapes*. Now, I don't know how many kids there are in the program, but we have a lot of them coming into our intensive internship program. They are really sharp, top-notch young adults. The industry is going to be well-served by the next generation."

Chateau Ste.
Michelle's welcoming
entrance

ENDLESS VINTAGES AND GOALS AHEAD

In 2017 Ste. Michelle Wine Estates is firmly established as one of the leading domestic wine brands sold in the United States. It is also the dominant leader in the Washington wine business, producing 8.2 million cases per year—a number that comprises two-thirds of the total amount of commercial wine made here. Over its first 50 years, the company has grown to once-unimaginable levels: It currently utilizes a dozen wine-making facilities, employs nearly 1,000 workers, and brings in around $700 million in annual revenues.

All told, Washington State wine production is now a $4.8 billion-plus industry, with over 60,000 acres planted to *vinifera* grapes and about 1,000 wineries. Only California surpasses Washington nationally in premium wine production—partially because it has ten times the acreage planted to *vinifera* grapevines.

Baseler believes even that imbalance will be altered over time. "There are, of course," he admits, "many wonderful wines in California. Napa, Sonoma, Central Coast, and other areas produce pretty spectacular wines. But I think in the long run we've got some advantages over California because of our weather, soil type, and potential water access." In this generally friendly state vs. state long game, the matter of physical space conducive to agriculture is truly worthy of consideration.

"If you look at the statistics right now," Baseler says, "there are about 600,000 acres of *vinifera* vines in California. We have about 60,000. So the ratio is ten to one. They are way ahead of us. I think in 15 to 20 years we'll be at over 200,000 acres. In total acreage, I doubt that we'll ever eclipse California, but in *premium* acres, I think it's possible that we'll have more. Which is very exciting because it will create jobs—good-paying jobs in the industry and also in tourism."

Some of the many keys to Ste. Michelle's success over the decades were the brilliant minds recruited into the fold along the way. Among the major contributors, André Tchelistcheff was a towering figure. As Doug Gore recently reflected, "One of the best things he did was bring up news from California and from his travels around the world. He told us what they were doing. How they were making wine. What we could learn from it. How we could get better. He was always very supportive. He could always answer a question. And he was ever-changing—for the right reasons. He was changing to get better… and because of new knowledge. For André, it was always: 'Keep an open mind. Don't be afraid of change. Seek it for the right reasons.'"

Gore also credits to Ted Baseler and the whole team. "When Ted became our leader, things accelerated. He really brought people together and made the place much more collegial. The relationship between Eastern and Western Washington became much tighter because of him. Ted deserves a lot of credit for making us who we are today. And I don't think we've ever had a better group of winemakers—they're passionate people who care about what goes on. We've never had better people, and we've never had better grapes."

Fall harvest at Canoe Ridge Estate

All that certainly helps reveal why this particular winery, in this once overlooked part of the country, managed to do the near-impossible when almost nobody could see it coming. "There's this chemistry term: 'energy of activation,'" offers Bob Betz as one explanation. "For example: Take the head of a match. You have all this energy bound up, but you must strike that against a jagged surface before that energy is released. With what we had in the vineyards and with the staff—it was energy of activation tied up at Chateau Ste. Michelle. It *needed* to be released. It was more evolutionary than revolutionary, but there was a moment that we hit where all of a

QUALITY

strict laboratory controls

You can assure your customers with the utmost confidence that the color, clarity, flavor and bouquet of Pommerelle wines are unsurpassed. One factor in Pommerelle's outstanding quality is the strict laboratory controls exercised throughout the production processes. From the day the raw materials are received until Pommerelle wines are bottled for shipment, tests are continually run for sugar, acid and alcohol content, metals, clarity, heat and cold stabilization and other factors that make a truly fine wine. The skill and everlasting care used in making Pommerelle wines have made them the largest selling Washington wines. It pays to sell the leader.

Science + passion = fine wines

sudden the spark ignited and we erupted onto the global scene. We snuck up on people. They didn't expect it. But the sheer energy that we released!"

As company founder Wally Opdycke reflected, "I think this whole thing was new territory for lots of people, and our team proved to be very capable of doing amazingly good things. It actually went far beyond even my own ambitions." Opdycke's successor, Allen Shoup, concurs [about the winery's remarkable successes]. "I can safely say that no one envisioned that we would be where we are today—and so quickly. We came from an unknown viticulture region, with no vineyards and no wineries. And in this very short span of time we've become world competitive."

Ted Baseler put it this way: "What's really unique about the history of this company is that we helped create and define an entire industry. Without Chateau Ste. Michelle, there would be wineries here and probably a very interesting hobby industry, but there wouldn't be 900 wineries. There wouldn't be global distribution of Washington wine to 100 countries. We contributed to creating an entire wine region. The philosophy of building the region and not worrying about market share has made that possible."

Throughout this past half-century of phenomenal accomplishments, Chateau Ste. Michelle has provided visionary leadership and unparalleled support that has helped spur the astounding ascendance of the Washington wine industry. It was a span of time that began in an era when there was still much to be learned about grapes and vineyard practices—many of our local wines were of questionable quality, and zero Washington wines were being shipped outside state lines.

We are now at a point in history where the Pacific Northwest's robust wine industry proudly stands on its own as witness to the fact that the greatest dreams of those earliest winemakers whose stories are told in this book have come true. The Washington wine business currently provides an estimated 27,000 grape- and wine-related jobs. Furthermore, Washington wine is now available in all 50 states (and over 100 countries worldwide) and is universally acknowledged as being of truly world-class stature. Sure, it took a few decades—albeit far less than the couple thousand years for Burgundy to attain its internationally revered status, or California's 100-plus years to get fully established. In hindsight, this regional transformation within 50 brief years remains simply breathtaking—as are many of the wines currently being crafted here in Washington.

Glorious grapes at the Viewcrest Vineyard in the Yakima Valley, sourced for many of the Eroica Rieslings

1930 TO 1979

1934-1935

Prohibition era ends. Two Seattle wine companies are established: **NAWICO** (National Wine Company) and **Pommerelle**. They produce mostly fruit wines.

1954

Pommerelle and NAWICO merge to become **American Wine Growers**, forming the largest winery in Washington State.

1967

American Wine Growers launches "**Ste. Michelle**" wines under the direction of legendary California winemaker and consultant André Tchelistcheff. Cabernet Sauvignon, Pinot Noir, Sémillon and Grenache Rosé are produced.

1972

Ste. Michelle begins planting 500 acres at **Cold Creek Vineyard** in Eastern Washington, which doubled the state's wine grape acreage at the time. The vineyard is one of the oldest and most iconic vineyards in Washington today.

1974

Los Angeles Times holds blind tasting of 19 White Rieslings. **Ste. Michelle's 1972 Riesling** ranks first. Winery is catapulted into national spotlight.

1976

Chateau Ste. Michelle's Woodinville "chateau" opens for winemaking and visitor tours. Label changes from Ste. Michelle Vintners to **Chateau Ste. Michelle**.

1980 TO 1999

1983

The River Ridge winery and vineyard is established on the banks of the Columbia River, later named **Columbia Crest**. Columbia Crest ultimately becomes one of the largest and most acclaimed wineries in Washington.

1986

Ste. Michelle acquires one of Napa Valley's most prestigious Cabernet Sauvignon wineries, **Conn Creek**.

1994

First vintage of **Northstar Merlot** is produced. The Northstar winery opens in Walla Walla, Washington, in 2002, dedicated to producing world-class Merlot.

1995

Chateau Ste. Michaelle partners with **Marchese Piero Antinori**, famed Italian winemaker, to release the first vintage of **Col Solare**, an internationally styled red wine from the Columbia Valley.

1999

Chateau Ste. Michelle joins **Ernst Loosen**, famed German winemaker, to harvest Washington grapes for a new high-end Riesling **Eroica**, and an ultra premium sweet wine (trockenbeerenauslese), called Single Berry Select. Eroica is named to *Wine Spectator*'s "Top 100" for its first five vintages.

2000 TO 2009

2004

Chateau Ste. Michelle is named 2004 **"American Winery of the Year"** by *Wine Enthusiast* magazine.

2005

New on-premises brand **14 Hands** from Washington State is launched. Consumer demand propels the brand to become the fastest growing Washington wine brand in history over the next decade.

Ste. Michelle Wine Estates acquires the highly acclaimed **Spring Valley Vineyard** outside of Walla Walla, Washington.

2006

State-of-the-art **Col Solare** winery is dedicated atop Red Mountain near Benton City, Washington.

Ste. Michelle Wine Estates acquires **Erath Winery**, one of the Willamette Valley's pioneering Pinot Noir producers, based in Dundee, Oregon.

Ste. Michelle Wine Estates forms a strategic alliance with the **Antinori family** to exclusively distribute their wines in the United States.

2007

Stag's Leap Wine Cellars of Napa Valley, one of the world's most highly regarded winery estates, is acquired by the joint venture partnership of Ste. Michelle Wine Estates and the Antinori family.

2009

Ste. Michelle Wine Estates is named U.S. importer for **Champagne Nicolas Feuillatte**, the No. 1 selling Champagne in France, along with ultra-luxury Champagne, Palmes d'Or.

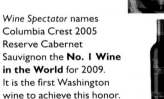

Wine Spectator names Columbia Crest 2005 Reserve Cabernet Sauvignon the **No. 1 Wine in the World** for 2009. It is the first Washington wine to achieve this honor.

2010 TO NOW

2010

Ste. Michelle Wine Estates is named U.S. importer for **Villa Maria Estates**, New Zealand's most awarded winery.

2014

14 Hands opens new winery in Prosser, Washington.

Ste. Michelle Wine Estates is appointed exclusive U.S. importer for the **Miguel Torres** family of wines from Spain and Chile.

2015

Chateau Ste. Michelle is named a **"Winery of the Year"** for the 21st time by *Wine & Spirits* magazine, more than any other American winery.

Ste. Michelle Wine Estates forms a collaboration with Rhône winemakers Michel Gassier and Philippe Cambie to help elevate Syrah from Washington with **Tenet Wines**. The flagship wine from Tenet receives **95 points** from The *Wine Advocate* in its first vintage.

Washington State University dedicates the **Ste. Michelle Wine Estates Wine Science Center,** a state-of-the art research and teaching institution for the Washington grape and wine industries.

Ted Baseler, president/CEO of Ste. Michelle Wine Estates since 2001, received the Lifetime Achievement Award from Southern Wine & Spirits of America.

2016

Ste. Michelle Wine Estates acquires **Patz & Hall Winery**, one of California's most highly regarded producers of single-vineyard Chardonnay and Pinot Noir.

ENDNOTES

1. Leon D. Adams, *The Wines of America*, 3rd ed. (Boston: Houghton Mifflin, 1973), 334.

2. Ronald Irvine with Walter J. Clore, *The Wine Project: Washington State's Winemaking History* (Vashon: Sketch Publications, 1997), 119.

3. Cynthia Stewart Kaag, "The Science of Wine: Washington State University Scientists and the Development of the Washington Wine Industry, 1937–1992," Ph.D. dissertation, December 2008, WSU Dept. of History, http://www.dissertations.wsu.edu/Dissertations/Fall2008/c_kaag_092908.pdf, 36 (accessed October 24, 2016).

4. Peter LeSourd, "Blue Laws—Washington State," http://www.historylink.org/File/9057 (accessed October 24, 2016).

5. Adams, *Wines of America*, 334.

6. "Scientific Quality Control Aids Modern Winemakers," *The Seattle Times*, November.15, 1953, C–11.

7. Kaag, *Science of Wine*, 2.

8. Ibid., v.

9. Ibid., 4.

10. Ibid., 4-5.

11. Ibid., 29.

12. "Man behind state's wine industry dies," obit, *Seattle Post-Intelligencer*, July 9, 2007, http://seattlepi.nwsource (accessed October 18, 2016).

13. Kaag, *Science of Wine*, 5.

14. Erwin Laurance, "Spirited New Machines Pep Up Wine-Bottling," *The Seattle Times*, October 15, 1961, 67.

15. Ibid.

16. Adams, *Wines of America*, 335.

17. Kaag, *Science of Wine*, 48.

18. "André Tchelistcheff," obit, *San Francisco Chronicle,* April 7, 1994, A–24.

19. Ronald Irvine and Walter J. Clore, *The Wine Project: Washington State's Winemaking History* (Sketch Publications, 1998), 204.

20. Adams, *Wines of America*, 336.

21. John Hinterberger, "Washington Wine: It's Not Bush," *The Seattle Times*, November 5, 1972, A-7.

22. Adams, *Wines of America*, 334.

23. Walter Clore, "A Brief History of Washington Wine: Washington Wine History, Part 1," WSU College of Agricultural, Human, and Natural Resource Sciences, http://cahnrs.wsu.edu/blog/2007/04/a-brief-history-of-washington-wine-walter-clore-washington-wine-history-part-1/ (accessed October 25, 2016).

24. Richard Kinssies, "On Wine: 30 Years of Chateau Ste. Michelle," http://seattlepi.nwsource.com (accessed September 6, 2006).

25. Irvine and Clore, *The Wine Project,* 236.

26. Tom Stockley, "Yakima Riesling Beats World's Best," *The Seattle Times*, October 30, 1974, E-2.

27. Kinssies, "On Wine."

28. *Pioneering Legacies: The Story of Hollywood Farm,* Chateau Ste. Michelle brochure, undated.

29. Polly Lane, "1912 Estate Becomes Showcase for Winery," *The Seattle Times,* September 14, 1975, D-1.

30. J. Elizabeth Purser & Lawrence J. Allen, *The Winemakers of the Pacific Northwest* (Vashon Island: Harbor House Publishing, 1977), 73.

31. Ted Jordan Meredith, *The Wines and Wineries of America's Northwest* (Kirkland: Nexus Press, 1986), 137.

32. Purser & Allen, *Winemakers of Pacific NW,* 73.

33. Ronald Holden & Glenda Holden, *Northwest Wine Country* (Seattle: Holden Pacific Inc., 1986), 9-10.

34. Kinssies, "On Wine."

35. Melissa Allison, "Wine World Toasts Ste. Michelle—Twin honors in Tough Times: Cabernet wins 'Wine of the Year,' CEO named 'Man of the Year',", *The Seattle Times*, January 11, 2010, A-1.

36. Blaine Schultz, "Model Gives Immigrant Eye-view of History," *The Seattle Times Magazine*, July 18, 1984, F-1.

37. Alf Collins, "Go East! Winery Has a Monumental Task," *The Seattle Times Magazine*, May 24, 1984, D-3.

38. George Dewan, "Helping The Lady Is Good Business," *The Wall Street Journal,* July 5, 1995, D-1.

39. Holden & Holden, *NW Wine Country,* 43.

40. Eric Degerman and Andy Perdue, "Sip a Bit of Washington Wine History with Whidbey's Port," Northwest Wine Press, http://www.winepressnw.com/2014/02/26/2847248_sip-a-bit-of-washington-wine-history.html?rh=1 (accessed February 26, 2014).

41. Andy Perdue, "John Sarich, Pioneer of NW Food and Wine," http://www.seattletimes.com/seattle-news/obituaries/john-sarich-pioneer-of-nw-food-and-wine/ (accessed October 6, 2014).

42. Patty Payne, "Community Mourns the Passing John Sarich, Star Chef and Longtime Culinary Director at Chateau Ste. Michelle," (http://www.bizjournals.com/seattle/blog/2014/10/community-mourns-the-passing-john-sarich-star-chef.html (accessed October 7, 2014).

43. Tom Stockley, "Things are Popping Out Like Corks from Champagne at Ste. Michelle," *The Seattle Times Magazine,* April 4, 1998, F-3.

44. "Antinori And Chateau Ste. Michelle Announce Winemaking Alliance," CSM press release, March 20, 1998.

45. Ibid.

46. "About Ernst Loosen: Profile of a Winemaker," dr.loosen.com (accessed December 20, 2016).

47. The Tenet.com (accessed December 20, 2016).

48. Kinssies, "On Wine"49. Andy Perdue, "Mike Januik Enjoys Success, Accolades from Long Winemaking Career," http://www.greatnorthwestwine.com/2016/07/21/mike-januik-podcast/ (accessed November 7, 2016).

50. Mike Ullmann, "The Man Who Saved Washington Wine," *Seattle Business,* June 2009, http://www.seattlebusinessmag.com/article/man-who-saved-washington-wine (accessed October 24, 2016).

51. Kinssies, "On Wine."

SOURCES

Author Interviews:

Baseler, Ted, October 13, 2016

Bertheau, Bob, December 2, 2016

Betz, Bob, November 10, 2016

Corliss, Kevin, October 31, 2016

Gore, Doug, October 31, 2016

Januik, Mike, November 9, 2016

Opdycke, Wally, November 12, 2016

Shoup, Allen, November 5, 2016

Simon, Kay, November 12, 2016

Newspapers & Magazines:

Patrick E. McGovern, "Wine's Prehistory – Wine for Eternity," *Archaeology*,
    July/August 1998, 32–34.

H.W. Margeson, "F.H.A. Reports Climb In Loans" *The Seattle Times*, September 2,
    1935, 15.

"Fast Transportation of Grapes Factor in Quality of N.W. Wine," *The Seattle Times*,
    November 15, 1953, C-7.

"Scientific Quality Control Aids Modern Winemakers," *Ibid.*,
    November 15, 1953, C-11.

Erwin Laurance, "Spirited New Machines Pep Up Wine-Bottling," *Ibid.*, October,
    15, 1961, 67.

John Hinterberger, "Washington Wine: It's Not Bush," *Ibid.*, November 5, 1972, A-7.

John J. Reddin, "Frank Sugia: Town's Most Unlikely Vegetable Gardener," *Ibid.*,
    May 4, 1972, B-7.

"State's Largest Wine Producer is Sold," *The Seattle Times*, May 10, 1973, F-10.

Tom Stockley, "Wine: Washington Can be Best in U.S.," *Ibid.*,
    September 26, 1973, E-5.

"U.S. Tobacco to Acquire State's Largest Vintner," *Ibid.*, October 4, 1973, H-4.

Tom Stockley, "Yakima Riesling Beats World's Best," *Ibid.*, October 30, 1974, E-2.

"U.S. Tobacco Acquires Seattle Vintner," *Ibid.*, February 21, 1974, B-6.

Polly Lane, "1912 Estate Becomes Showcase for Winery," *Ibid.*,
    September 14, 1975, D-1.

"Victor B. Allison, Wine Executive, Dies," *Ibid.*, September 30, 1977, E-6.

Tom Stockley, "Washington's Biggest Winery Updates Image," *Ibid.*,
    April 7, 1976, E-2.

Peter Rinearson, "Ahh, Woodinville '76 – Winery to be Decanted This Month,"
    Ibid., August 11, 1976, H-10.

Tom Stockley, "Tom Stockley on Wineries in Washington," *The Seattle Times
    Magazine,* May 1, 1977, 8.

"Victor B. Allison, Wine Executive, Dies," *Ibid.*, September 30, 1977, E-6.

Alf Collins, "Go East! Winery Has a Monumental Task," *Ibid.*, May 24, 1984, D-3.

Sally Gene Mahoney, "For First Time, State Government is Promoting
    Washington Wines, *Ibid.*, June 10, 1984, D-1-3.

Blaine Schultz, "Model Gives Immigrant Eye-view of History," *Ibid.*,
    July 18, 1984, F-1.

Tom Stockley, "Once a Trickle in the Industry, State Wineries Now Make a Splash,"
    Ibid., March 27, 1985, E-8.
Herb Robinson, "Washington's Wine Industry Needs Help," *Ibid*.,
    February 8, 1987, A-18.
Louis T. Corsaletti, "Winery's Not out of Woods Yet on Zoning," *Ibid*.,
    June 4, 1987, B-1.
Steve Johnston, "Concert at Woodinville Winery Could be Corked – Court May
    Temporarily Halt Ste. Michelle Events," *Ibid*., July 23, 1987, B-2.
Addy Hatch, "'No Compromise' Philosophy Brings Honor to Winery," *Ibid*.,
    October 31, 1988, F–2.
Scott Williams, "A Vintage Battle—Farmworkers' Long Struggle With Ste. Michelle
    Winery Has a Twist: Management Wants a Law That Gives Farmworkers the
    Right to Bargain," *Ibid*., October 4, 1992, A-1.
Geordie Wilson, "Music Notes," *Ibid*., August 6, 1993, D-4.
Tom Stockley, "Things are Popping Out Like Corks from Champagne at
    Ste. Michelle," *Ibid*., April 4, 1998, F-3.
Tom Stockley, "Collaboration Debuts and It's a Blockbuster," *Ibid*., April 7, 1999, F-4.
Thomas P. Skeen, "'Dream Team' Joins Forces in Launching State Wineries," *Ibid*.,
    March 1, 2003, B-2.
Melissa Allison, "Wine World Toasts Ste. Michelle —Twin Honors in Tough Times:
    Cabernet Wins 'Wine of the Year,' CEO Named 'Man of the Year'," *Ibid*.,
    January 11, 2010, A-1.
Jon Talton, "Outlining the Business of Washington Wines," *Ibid*., March 17, 2013, D-5.
"High Price of Wine," *Seattle Post-Intelligencer*, July 25, 1969, 6.
Stan Reed, "Gourmet Spoken Here," *Ibid*., August 17, 1970, 11.
"André Tchelistcheff," obit, *San Francisco Chronicle* April 7, 1994, A-24.
G. Pascal Zachary, "Winery's Field Workers Break New Ground in Union Election,"
    The Wall Street Journal, June 7, 1995, B-1, B-8.
George Dewan, "Helping the Lady is Good Business," *Ibid*., July 5, 1995, D-1.
Howard S. Goldberg, "Leon Adams, Wine Expert and Writer, 90," obit,
    http://www.nytimes.com (accessed October 24, 2016).
Harvey Steiman, "Washington an Open Secret—World-class Wines Flow from this
    Unheralded Quality Frontier," Wine Spectator, December 15, 2010.

Books & Misc. Printed Materials:
Murray Morgan, *Puget's Sound: A Narrative of Early Tacoma and the Southern Sound*
    (University of Washington Press, 1979), 5–6, 29.
Robert T. Reid, "Growing and Marketing of Grapes," *Monthly Bulletin*,
    Western Washington Experiment Station, Puyallup, March 1918, 174–77.
Fred Stimson, "The Story of Hollywood Farm,"
    (Seattle: Fred S. Stimson Co., 1919), 1–11.
Pioneering Legacies: The Story of Hollywood Farm, Chateau Ste. Michelle brochure,
    undated.
Carl H. Kroll, "Pommerelle and I," Handwritten Memoir Letter, July 2001
    (courtesy CSM archives).
Lloyd S. Woodburne, *Associated Vintners: The First Twenty Years*, unpublished
    manuscript, UW Special Collections (Accession # 3461-001).
Leon D. Adams, *The Wines of America*, 3rd ed. (Boston: Houghton Mifflin, 1973),
    334–39.

Ronald Irvine with Walter J. Clore, *The Wine Project: Washington State's Winemaking History* (Vashon: Sketch Publications, 1997), 21, 149–51,161–65, 180–85, 235–36, 240–41, 294–99, 301, 360–78.

Norman H. Clark, *The Dry Year—Prohibition & Social Change in Washington* (Seattle: University of Washington Press, 1988), 258–60.

J. Elizabeth Purser & Lawrence J. Allen, *The Winemakers of the Pacific Northwest* (Vashon Island: Harbor House Publishing, 1977), 72–75, 106–23.

Bob Betz, *Tastes of Liberty—A Celebration of our Great Ethnic Cooking* (New York: Stewart, Tabori & Chang, 1985).

Ted Jordan-Meredith *The Wines and Wineries of America's Northwest* (Kirkland: Nexus Press, 1986), 134–38.

Ronald Holden & Glenda Holden, *Northwest Wine Country* (Seattle: Holden Pacific Inc., 1986), 40–46.

Ted Jordan-Meredith, *Northwest Wine: Winegrowing Alchemy Along the Pacific Ring of Fire* (Kirkland: Nexus Press, 1990), 158–61.

Sen. Patty Murray, "Tribute To Walter Clore," *Congressional Record*, Vol.149, No.36, March 6, 2003.

Paul Gregutt, *Washington Wines & Wineries: The Essential Guide* (Berkeley and Los Angeles: University of California Press, 2007), 16, 122–23.

Ronald Holden, *Forking Seattle* (Seattle: Holden, 2016), 179, 181.

Websites:

"About Ernst Loosen: Profile of a Winemaker," dr.loosen.com (accessed December 20, 2016).

TheTenet.com (accessed December 20, 2016).

Washington State Wine Commission, https://www.washingtonwine.org/ (accessed October 1, 2016).

"A Brief History of Washington Wine: Walter Clore–Washington Wine History, Part 1," http://cahnrs.wsu.edu/blog/2007/04/a-brief-history-of-washington-wine-walter-clore-washington-wine-history-part-1/ (accessed October 25, 2016).

Cynthia Stewart Kaag, "The Science of Wine: Washington State University Scientists and the Development of the Washington Wine Industry, 1937-1992," Ph.D. dissertation, December 2008, http://www.dissertations.wsu.edu/Dissertations/Fall2008/c_kaag_092908.pdf (accessed October 24, 2016).

Peter Blecha, "Wine in Washington," http://www.historylink.org/ (accessed October 2, 2016).

Andy Perdue, "Washington's Wine History: A Confederate soldier, Prohibition and a Vine Planted in 1872," http://www.seattletimes.com/pacific-nw-magazine/old-vines-tell-the-story-of-washingtons-rich-wine-history/

"The Letters and Journals of Narcissa Whitman: 1836–1847," http://www.pbs.org/weta/thewest/resources/archives/two/whitman1.htm

Nick Tomassi, "'Island Belle' Has Roots in History," http://web.kitsapsun.com/archive/1998/11-04/0093_wine_cabinet___island_belle_has_r.htm (accessed October 24, 2016).

Peter LeSourd, "Blue Laws—Washington State," http://www.historylink.org/File/9057 (accessed October 24, 2016).

"Man Behind State's Wine Industry Dies," http://seattlepi.nwsource (accessed October 24, 2016).

Seattle Civil Rights & Labor History Project, "Timeline: Farm Worker Organizing in Washington State," http://depts.washington.edu/civilr/farmwk_timeline.htm (accessed November 1, 2016).

Oscar Rosales Castañeda, "The Creation of the Washington State UFW in the 1980s," Seattle Civil Rights & Labor History Project http://depts.washington.edu/civilr/farmwk_ch9.htm (accessed November 3, 2016).

Richard Kinssies, "On Wine: 30 Years of Chateau Ste. Michelle," http://seattlepi.nwsource.com (accessed October 24, 2016).

Tom Stockley, "Something To Hoot About: The Dinner Train," http://community.seattletimes.nwsource.com/archive/?date=19920513&slug=1491588 (accessed November 1, 2016).

"Ste. Michelle Wine Estates Acquires Acclaimed Vineyard in Oregon's Eola-Amity Hills for Erath Winery," https://www.erath.com/winery/newsDetail/311 (accessed November 7, 2016).

"Willakia Purchased," http://www.oregonwinepress.com/willakia-purchased-0414 (accessed November 1, 2016).

Patty Payne, "Community Mourns the Passing of John Sarich, Star Chef and Longtime Culinary Director at Chateau Ste. Michelle," http://www.bizjournals.com/seattle/blog/2014/10/community-mourns-the-passing-john-sarich-star-chef.html (accessed October 24, 2016).

Andy Perdue, "John Sarich, Pioneer of NW Food and Wine," http://www.seattle-times.com/seattle-news/obituaries/john-sarich-pioneer-of-nw-food-and-wine/ (accessed October 6, 2014).

Andy Perdue, "Mike Januik enjoys success, accolades from long winemaking career," http://www.greatnorthwestwine.com/2016/07/21/mike-januik-podcast/ (accessed November 7, 2016).

"John Sarich: In Memoriam," https://www.ste-michelle.com/about-us/john-sarich-scholarship (accessed October 27, 2016).

Leslie Kelly, "Alex Golitzen, Quilceda Creek," http://quilcedacreek.com/articles/washingtonwine-alex-golitzin.aspx (accessed November 1, 2016).

Ronald Holden, "The Gospel According To Joel Butler," http://edibleseattle.com/the-gospel-according-to-joel/ (accessed October 23, 2016).

"WSU opens new Ste. Michelle Wine Science Center," http://cahnrs.wsu.edu/blog/2015/06/wsu-dedicates-new-ste-michelle-wine-science-center/ (accessed October 24, 2016).

Mike Ullmann, "The Man Who Saved Washington Wine," http://www.seattlebusinessmag.com/article/man-who-saved-washington-wine (accessed October 23, 2016).

Eric Degerman and Andy Perdue, "Sip a bit of Washington Wine History with Whidbey's Port," http://www.winepressnw.com/2014/02/26/2847248_sip-a-bit-of-washington-wine-history.html?rh=1 (accessed November 7, 2016).

Eric Degerman and Andy Perdue, "Yakima Valley vineyard's 100-year history," http://www.heraldnet.com (accessed March 3, 2016).

"Howard Somers," obit, http://web.kitsapsun.com/archive/2005/01-19/27803_howard_somers.html (accessed October 24, 2016).

PHOTO CREDITS

AUTHOR'S ACKNOWLEDGMENTS

It is an old, old saying—perhaps as ancient as a forgotten amphora of Roman vino—yet it remains true: Any writer's job is made much easier if the story being told is a robust one. Well, lucky me. The saga behind the rise of Chateau Ste. Michelle is precisely that. The public unveiling of the Chateau facility itself back in 1976 was such a big deal regionally that the media hoopla even caught the attention of this then-20-year-old beer-sipping UW history undergrad. News coverage about the winery's grand opening events sparked a real sense of excitement. But little could anyone have known that the occasion was such a major milestone, indeed a turning point, in the state's wine history. It took time to appreciate all that. But four decades later when the opportunity arose to pen this book, Chateau Ste. Michelle's long string of achievements became clear.

This story of the emergence and maturing of Washington's most important winery, and the vision of its leaders, is a dynamic one and my work greatly benefitted from the time that numerous wine luminaries generously shared with me. I am particularly grateful to current and former Chateau Ste. Michelle staff-members including: Wally Opdycke, Allen Shoup, Ted Baseler, Bob Betz, Mike Januik, Doug Gore, Kevin Corliss, Kay Simon, Bob Bertheau, Lynda Eller, Megan Ayers, Joan Fennell, Carole Viney, and Ann Hunt.

Deep gratitude also to HistoryLink.org Executive Director Marie McCaffrey for helping plant the seed of this book idea, and to Editorial Director Petyr Beck and his Documentary Media team for gently guiding it to fruition.

Lastly, I want to thank my wife, Kate Race, for accompanying me on so many great wine tour adventures, and also Jay Schiering, Dan McCarthy, and the whole crew at Seattle's McCarthy & Schiering Wine Merchants for welcoming me onto their team and providing the opportunity to explore further the wide world of the wine business.

INDEX